Growth Hacking for Hair Salons
Transform Your Hair Salon, Day Spa or Service Business Into a Badass Money Machine!

250+ Growth Hacks to Get More Traffic and Sales

Grow Your Profits Quickly and Cost Effectively

Linda L. Chappo

Growth Hacking for Hair Salons:
Transform Your Hair Salon, Day Spa or Service Business
Into a Badass Money Machine!
250 Growth Hacks to Get More Traffic and Sales

DEDICATION

This book is dedicated to every visionary
who seeks to grow her or his business
quickly and cost effectively!

Other Business Books by Linda L. Chappo

**Growth Hacking for Beginners;
How to Transform Your Business Into
A Badass Money Machine**

How to Start UP and Manage Your Own Hair Salon
and Make it BIG in the Salon Business

How to Organize Your Marketing Campaign
and Hit the Ground Running

Full Strength Marketing
How You Can Use Your Hidden Strength,
Break Through Inner Barriers, and Raise Your Profits
By Linda L. Chappo & Tom Marcoux

TABLE OF CONTENTS

We invite you to leave an honest review on Amazon.com or on the web site of any vendor where you made your purchase.

***

Contact us at:

businessacademy10@aol.com

for free online learning experiences.

INTRODUCTION

It's What You Know and Do That Makes
You Successful in Business

Educational events and hairdresser conferences were a huge part of my long cosmetology career. I felt it was important to learn as much as I could, not only for myself, but for my salon and my employees. Our success depended upon my confidence as a marketer and leader.

At a conference in Chicago, a platform speaker blatantly said that "most salon owners are in a coma!" That comment towards the women and men in my industry angered me. He went on to explain how we fail to take action toward marketing and leadership. If you own a salon, you are no longer just a hairdresser. Your position has changed dramatically. You are a marketer, leader, and business person.

From that day forth I stepped up to the plate and went beyond wishing, hoping and praying for more customers. It's critical to educate ourselves and take action. We need to let our communities know we exist and we can help them with their hair, skin and nail problems. This book is the culmination of my efforts to have successful salons. I trust that you'll appreciate this gift.

If you have a hair salon or service business and need to grow it quickly and cost effectively, then growth hacking is the right marketing strategy for you. No experience? No problem! You'll learn 250+ growth hacks to help you turn your business into a *Badass Money Machine!*

The basics and principles of smart marketing have not changed in any significant way, but the platforms used on a daily basis have changed due to the popularity of the internet and the advent of social media platforms.

Growth Hacking for Hair Salons will cover cost effective ways to be seen on social media platforms along with traditional media marketing. Social media platforms opened up a whole new world of advertising opportunities and varied ways to reach your target audience. While marketing to pull in more customers has gotten more complicated and time consuming, it's also more fun.

You could call social media marketing *relationship marketing* in the truest sense of the term. In order to create that *Badass Buzz* that we all dream about, and keep customers coming back, you need to build excellent relationships and maintain them through-out the years. You'll learn about how to do that with this book.

What I've comprised and compiled in this book is many years of marketing experience from the old days, (which for me is 1975+) and is still totally valid. Also included is a valuable investigation of current social media platforms.

Unlike the standard marketing outlets like direct mail, radio, television, billboards, flyers, press releases etc., which will always be utilized on some level (Apple and Microsoft use extensive television and billboard advertising), know that internet marketing via social media will change pretty much on a daily basis. That's both the good news and the bad news! The good news is that there will always be more opportunities for growth, and the bad news is that you have to keep up and there is always a learning curve. I know, ugh!

For a more detailed and personal education you will be directed to online courses that are taught by experts in their field. Our affiliate partner, CreativeLive, offers expert online courses in business, creativity and life. *We may be compensated if you purchase a course.*

We all know that learning is a lifelong process, especially when you own a salon or service business. You can take your skills to the next level through our valuable email newsletter: businessacademy10@aol.com It's full of useful information and freebies!

BusinessAcademy.com blog is the best place to go for

upgrading your business skills with top educators: sales, marketing, creative, branding, social media, public relations and more.

Marketing and promoting your business is like planting seeds. Sometimes those seeds sprout activity right away and other times the seed grows slow or not at all. There are reasons for the way a community responds to a certain industry, field or innovation. Your product or service may or may not be right for that person. Maybe it's not right for them today, but it might be right for them in a week or a month or a year. That's why it's so important to be consistent in your marketing efforts and learn new technologies from the pro's. Your name will come up when customers need what you have.

As small business owners, you can make a big splash on social media when you let your personality shine through your content: blogs, podcasts, videos and advertisements. The costs for advertising on social platforms are less, but you will spend an inordinate amount of time creating content that speaks to and attracts your target market.

It's noisy out there in the marketplace, and this book is designed to help you cut through the noise, and choose the best platforms for your salon. It doesn't matter if you have a hair salon, a website and a blog, or just a salon. Everything you need is right here.

You are given lots of ways to attract customers in your neighborhood, community or online around the world, even if you are not a technological whiz or graphic designer.

Be patient as you read through this content and take notes, fill in the blanks, and use your creative mind to *Transform Your Hair Salon Into A Badass Money Machine!*

CHAPTER ONE:

BECOMING THE BADASS ENTREPRENEUR
It's All About Creating a Badass Buzz!

Are you a new hair salon, barber shop or nail salon or a stagnant business wanting to get your share of profits, traffic and worldwide exposure for your product or service? If it's attention that you seek, then you are in the right place. Everybody or almost everybody seems to be doing something online to make money or get noticed as an influencer. They want to create a *Badass Buzz!*

In the last ten years or so promoting one's hair or nail business has gotten more complicated. There is not only the traditional media (television, radio, billboards, direct mail etc.) to understand, but also massive online platforms to master. Many business owners are in the same shoes and we aring all the same hats. You're just starting out with no or few customers and having to do everything yourself: the legal aspects, marketing plans and execution, product or service innovations, payroll and on and on. It can seem overwhelming unless you have a *Badass* team to help you. Do you have a team? Can you create one, either locally or virtually?

Whether your hair/nail business has an online presence or not, you have double duty to do if you have a storefront/website and employees. You may be competing in a marketplace where existing businesses already have a big head start on you. They've mastered the marketing game years ago and now you have to play catch up. All is not lost. You and your business can catch up but there is a learning curve and I'm here to help you get up to speed through growth hacking i.e. growing your business as quickly, efficiently and cost effectively as possible. Do that and YOU can *Transform Your Hair Salon Into a Badass Money Machine.*

***

I'm going to be honest with you. Your first two years are the most crucial. How you handle those two+ years will determine if more years will follow. It's that important. You need to create a *Badass Buzz!* I will give you plenty of tools and instruction, but most importantly I will give you 250+ ideas that can be implemented when you need them. You will know what your options are and what to do next.

With massive amounts of competition, it is more important than ever to use *growth hacking* and *establish a brand* in order to stand out from the crowd and be the ONE to get happily noticed. Handled correctly, you could be the one making profits, especially if you *tackle your niche first.* I'll talk about that a little later.

You need a *Badass* campaign or a plan for your start up or small business. In chapters two and three you will build a rock solid plan to take your business to the *Pinnacle of Success* (my publishing brand). Throughout these chapters you will learn the many aspects of *growth hacking* before the word/idea was ever coined. In this chapter you'll learn the benefits of *growth hacking* and why all new businesses are doing it to be successful.

What is a Growth Hacker?

A *growth hacker* is a business marketer who restricts their marketing activities primarily to growth. This is exactly what every start up salon needs in the beginning stages of their business. The *growth hacker* uses their limited resources (financial and manpower/ladypower) to grow their business quickly and cost effectively. We all want that, don't we? I've always said, "It's *a jungle out there, so we need to plan, prepare and proceed!"* Always remember that!

Growth hacking is also a way or system of using analytics and metrics to track people coming to your website or blog to purchase your products or services, or get information. It's important to see what you are doing that is effective. Ask those important questions and discover the answers. Are people reading certain blogs topics? Are they clicking on certain website pages looking for information to help them? If they're not *clicking* or *liking*, or spending any time there then you have more work to do.

Make some crucial tweaks or changes to your site, your business model, your branding or your business as a whole to see what works. You should be consistently testing your marketing materials or *the words you use* that attract your target audience. That is the value of analytics or *behind the scenes* numbers, and *numbers don't lie!* With literally the world at your doorstep (with cash or credit card in hand) it is important to know where you stand.

If you don't pay attention to this, you will unfortunately end up near the bottom of your category in the search engines where no one will find you. People don't have the time or the energy to scroll through hundreds of businesses that do exactly what you do to find you.

You must differentiate your business from others (through branding), try new methods to get noticed and track your progress *behind the scenes*. It's all there for you to see, and you'll find that information when you set up your business ads on social media platforms.

In the days where only traditional marketing methods existed (which are still important to use, but often more expensive), it was a bit easier to track the results of your advertising, promotions and publicity. You could tell who was walking through your door, calling on the phone, buying products off your shelves or tracking the stores that carried your product. If you sell your beauty products online, you'll see that business has changed all that to some degree because the whole *Badass Enchilada* is virtual, so learning how to navigate the

3

peaks and valleys of the digital highway is critical.

What Will Growth Hacking Do For YOUR Business?

I'll teach you about the tools and resources, tactics and strategies that are available for you on the internet that are either free or low cost. Plus you will get a little education in traditional marketing. I have another ebook that will help you with traditional marketing, *How to Organize Your Marketing Campaign, and Hit the Ground Running*, available on Amazon.com.

The real *Badass* advantage of learning this information is that you are offered 250 promotional ideas (which is the focus of this book) that can be used in your neighborhood location, and carry it over to a digital format.

The Internet Super Highway really is an endless digital highway of traffic where users (I really dislike that word) can make a pit stop at your business and buy what they need, whether it's your new cosmetic line, a unique piece of jewelry you've just started carrying, or your private label products. A click of a button and there they are, looking for you to solve their hair, skin or nail problem.

Most salon or nail business owners soon discover that they need to be a part of both worlds. They don't want to leave that money on the table, so they just go with the learning curve. The internet is a good, often fun, but sometimes mysterious tool for reaching out into the entire world for customers and profits.

The goal here is to take the mystery out of the whole damn process. That's what *Badass Growth Hackers* do. They become somewhat of a detective and learn what it takes to become a marketing genius. They learn the ropes, experiment with ideas, be open to creative inspiration, tackle risk and move forward one step at a time. They also stay current with their reading.

Along the way *growth hackers* look for successful role models, create a winning plan or roadmap, and accept those occasional bumps in the road as part of the journey. It doesn't matter if your business is with hair, nails, massage, tanning or internet retailer, just keep taking those steps until you get to the top of your industry.

What Is a *Badass* Entrepreneur and Are YOU One?

A *Badass* entrepreneur is a proactive business owner who is not in a proverbial coma when it comes to marketing or promoting their work or their business. The *Badass* isn't shy when it comes to networking, attending events, speaking in public or pitching to investors. It doesn't matter if the investor is a friend, family member or a venture capitalist. They know they have to do it, so they are prepared with their most effective pitch. The *Badass* promotes his or her business, product, service or website in public when it's appropriate to do so.

I've often claimed (in public) to be *a shameless self-promoter*. I once attended a business networking event at my local city hall. I stood up to briefly introduce myself, and just before finishing I held up my book, *"How to Start UP and Manage Your Own Hair Salon and Make it BIG in the Salon Business,"* (even though I figured there would be few or no hairstylists in attendance). I proudly admitted to everyone that, *"I was a shameless self-promoter."* After the meeting ended, most of the group rushed over to speak with me. For the first time ever, I felt like a celebrity (and it was all because I wrote a business book). When the opportunity arises, I go for it, and so should you!

Here's What the Badass Salon Business Owner Doesn't Do

This is called business etiquette. He or she doesn't take all the available time for him or herself at business networking events without giving others the chance to speak. Instead ¦of being a *Badass*, he or she is a hog, and no one likes a talking hog, a road hog or a time hog. He or she doesn't overpower others with what they know (unless they are being paid for their knowledge), and knows when to keep their *Badass* mouth on vibrate mode and just *"listen!"* I'm not saying the *Badass* business owner should play small, not at all! Play fair and be respectful of others.

Can YOU Be Proactive?

You provide massive value, so get yourself out there, and offer your products or services or both to people who need your help. Serve where you are needed. If you aren't proactive, you are in a proverbial coma, and that doesn't serve your business, your employees, your potential customers or your bottom line.

Expert Online Resource:
BusinessAcademy.com and their affiliate partner, CreativeLive, offers an online learning experience to teach you exactly how to win at getting traffic and sales.

Sales, Sales, Sales: Why People Buy by Tamara Lackey

This course covers the nuts and bolts of achieving great sales but goes far beyond, with the intention of priming you to consistently sell your work for what it's truly worth - and to create even better relationships with clients who will appreciate a better experience. If you own your own small business, you are in a 100% sales commission job.

Tamara will show you exactly how she maintains a consistently high sales average in multiple genres, sharing how to conquer fear of criticism and self-doubt and she will showcase what works, what doesn't, and how you may be killing your sales! Thumbs up by CreativeLive. BusinessAcademy may be compensated if you purchase a course.

* Copy this link into your browser: http://shrsl.com/1f8xf

* As the owner of BusinessAcademy.com, along with *growth hacking*, I can offer the entrepreneur and small salon business owner an invaluable online education for growing the business of their dreams through traditional and digital marketing methods and both digital and printed content. I'll include valuable resources as we go along.

Badass Important Tip #1: Get Rich in Your Niche!
One of the best places to *Transform Your Hair Salon Into a Badass Money*

Machine is in your niche. Let's answer some important questions.

1. What industry have you been working in the longest? Hair, Skincare, Nails, Retail Products?
2. Do you know all the in's and out's of your industry?
3. Do you know the problems that plague your industry and how to solve them?
4. Do you have connections in your industry that could provide support for you or teach you more of what is needed in the industry?

If you answered, "YES!" to all of these questions, then you can get rich or at least make some decent money. You might even have two built in audiences: the people in your niche, and the people your niche serves. You may also be able to carry that information over to another industry and create a more massive passive income.

You have valuable information that could help other people. So, what do you do with that info? You could write books, eBooks, online courses, webinars, public speaking, consulting or coaching or anything else you can think of, besides your regular work in your industry. Taking on extra work or another business is called *a side hustle.*

My side hustle: When I started my first hair salon in 1975, I couldn't find any books to specifically help me promote my business. I found books for other industries, but not mine. I studied them anyway and learned a lot. When I sold that salon I started to write the book I wish I had when I started: *"How to Start UP and Manage Your Own Hair Salon, and Make it BIG in the Salon Business."* I wrote about everything I learned, as well as my mistakes.

I eventually self-published the book when I discovered CreateSpace (now KDP/Amazon). I was a graphic designer at the time, so I created my own cover/layout and cover content. I made money right away, and continue to receive royalty income. I was NOT hearing crickets like many freelance writers. I wrote specifically for my niche, and they needed to hear about my valuable experiences that could guide them to success. I spent a lot of time and money attending classes and conferences over the years. You have to stay at the top of your game!

As a side note, I saved that money, and years later used a portion of my royalties to start up my third hair salon in Northern California. My ROI (Return on Investment) was through the roof.

The three things that set me on this lucrative writing course was 1) I had plenty of real world experience in the industry, 2) I had at least one really awesome referral that spoke to hairdressers and salon owners alike and 3) I knew all the pitfalls and how to solve them.

In fact, my plan is to tweak this book for the salon industry, and supply my niche with more great marketing ideas. I have a niche audience that know me and trust me to steer them correctly. Think about starting with your niche, and branch out from there.

Determine Your Brand and Build Your Tribe!

Branding is a cohesive strategy that determines how unique your business is through mission, aesthetics and execution across the board. Having a distinctive and compelling *brand* is one of the most important aspects of business success! "What is my brand?" should be one of the first questions you ask yourself as you start thinking through and putting together your new, or old revived business. It's that important to help you stand out in the world marketplace and give you what realtors call *Curb Appeal!*

When it comes to *Transforming Your Hair Salon Into a Badass Money Machine,* your first order of the day (after the legalities are complete) is to establish your brand's esthetics: colors, images, type of content, products, services … all based on speaking to and fulfilling the needs of your ideal customer.

For example: You have a name that sings to them, and a look that appeals to them. You have products, services and content that solves their problems and provides value at a price they can afford or are willing to pay.

Having a cohesive brand and a strategic plan is about empowering customers and alleviating any fears of being ripped off mentally, emotionally or financially. You're building a relationship based on trust, not on what customers buy or don't buy.

Build the relationship first and they will buy because they've become your *Tribe*! They know you and like you. People want to belong in order to gain support and fellowship. That's the beauty of social media: creating your own tribe, loyal followers that trust you to always provide whatever it is that you do best.

Study Your Competitor's Brands!

One of the most *Badass* important actions you can take is to study a number of your competitors and their brands. How have they branded themselves in a way that is dynamic? What is their message, their theme, and their energy? What images do they use to reach out and grab customer's attention? And what does it all say about them as a public servant, because that's what they are. And you are too. Through your branding efforts you are self-identifying as a servant, a problem solver, a like-minded buddy, and ultimately *a Happiness Maker.*

Become a Happiness Maker!

Whether I am going to a particular small business to get a haircut, a manicure, a facial, a bottle of shampoo or a new hair-color … leaving there *happy* is a big part of the equation for me. If I'm searching online for products to make my fingernails stronger … well, again I'm *happier* if I easily and effortlessly find those answers, and it all works out well for me. My day is made (more or less), and I can sleep at night.

That's what people want: no drama, no stress, no confusion, no hassle, no frustration and no voice mail hell! Here's the mantra that many people are chanting whether they verbalize it or not, *"Help me with what I need so I can get on with my day!"* We all have way too much to do, unfortunately!

9

Establishing your unique brand should be part of your initial business plan and marketing campaign. Remember your mission statement. Creating and sharing your mission statement with your audience builds a common bond. You speak to what customers care about, and that's a bridge to a better and stronger relationship.

***

The Crucial Details of this Book - Throughout the first four chapters you'll learn the importance of branding, targeted content, your website, marketing strategies, providing value, demographics, your logo, choosing the right social media platforms, and speaking to those ideal customers in a way that attracts them and doesn't repel them.

Chapters five through eleven will give you more than enough marketing ideas from which to choose, based on what will help you reach your ideal client. You will find both social media and traditional media options. The final chapter twelve will engage you in the problems, set backs and challenges that many entrepreneurs face and how you might solve them.

Throughout this entire training, you'll be exposed to online educational learning experiences. These online courses are taught by experts in their field and offered by our affiliate partner, CreativeLive. These courses are intended to give you a deeper understanding of the material presented here. CreativeLive also offers learning experiences in creativity, life, finances and personal development. I may be compensated for any course you purchase. Here is the Creativelive link for classes: Check Out CreativeLive's Free On-Air Classes

Expert Online Resource:
BusinessAcademy.com and their affiliate partner, CreativeLive, offers an online learning experience to teach you exactly how to win at getting traffic and sales.

"Branding Strategies to Grow Your Business"
by Jasmine Star

To learn more about effective branding, look on the www.businessacademy.com website for courses that can guide you through the process. Jasmine coaches you (ideally the entrepreneur with two to three years of experience) on how to reach the next phase of your business.

Get ready to feel genuinely excited again about your business, and build momentum by learning how to brand your business.

* BusinessAcademy may be compensated if you purchase a course.

• Identification of your brand voice
• Website, social media, and design alignment
• Effective copy strategies
• Basic principles of website design for optimal results

* Copy this link into your browser: http://shrsl.com/1f8t5

Notes:

USE WHAT YOU LEARNED IN CHAPTER ONE:
Becoming the Badass Entrepreneur;
It's all About the Badass Buzz!

1. What's at stake when you start a business!
2. The value of Growth Hacking!
3. What it takes to be a Badass entrepreneur!
4. How to get rich in your niche!
5. The importance of branding!
6. Two opportunities for expert online learning experiences.

Notes:

CHAPTER TWO:

KNOW WHERE YOU STAND
Getting Up to Speed with Assets and Liabilities

The Socrates quote, *"To know thyself is the beginning of wisdom"* is inspirational to many people, and may be considered the first rule of good marketing. And while you're getting to know yourself, you might as well get to know your business, customer and competition. That's what this chapter is all about. If you skip over it, you will be sorry, because this information is the foundation of your success.

In order to be successful at online or offline marketing, there are a number of things you need to know to get up to speed, and knowing as much as possible will help you make a larger impact with the time, money and effort that is required. Create for yourself an awareness of everything you have to work with … in other words what are your business's tangible and intangible assets and liabilities?

Create a Plan
Know where you are, and what it will take to get you where you want to go … success, profits, or community recognition! Define your destination, then plan the steps to get there. Use a visualization process to actually see where it is you want to go. See, in your mind's eye, the outcome of all your hard work. Then start with clearly defined baby

steps to get to that outcome.

Expert Online Resource:
BusinessAcademy.com and our affiliate, CreativeLive, offer an
expert online learning experience to guide you in building a
successful roadmap for your business.

Creating Your Ultimate Business Plan by Caroline Rogoll

A business plan is an essential roadmap for business success. Carolina Rogoll has been successfully leading small and large businesses, and building brands for over a decade.

In this short class, she will be walking you step-by-step on how to create a business plan using the easy-to-use template she has put together. By the end of this class, you will have a business plan you can share, reference, and start using right away. BusinessAcademy may be compensated if you purchase a course.

* Copy this link in your browser: http://shrsl.com/1f8fk

Get Up to Speed!
Answer these questions to the best of your ability, and if you have
the digital version of this book, simply write your answers into a
notebook or your business journal:

DEFINE YOUR BUSINESS

1. What exactly does your business do?
2. What is your mission statement?
3. Did you create a business plan or a guide to your success?
4. Is your marketing plan or campaign already completed for this
   year?

5. What are your short-term goals, one year?

6. What are your long-term goals, 5-10 years?

7. What is your vision, and how do you plan to implement it?

8. What is your niche?

9. Why did you choose that niche?

10. Do you have clarity on where your business is headed?

11. What problem(s) does your business solve?

12. What are your primary products, services or content?

13. What are the benefits of coming to your store or website and purchasing products/services?

14. How does your product or service now help your current customers?

15. Will your product or service change their lives?

16. If so, how?

17. Can your product or service be improved?

18. What would it take to improve it?

19. Is your product or service positioned at the right price for your target market?

20. Do you have a strategy for lifting customers to a higher price point, the upsell?

21. Is your online business a mirror image of your offline business?

22. Have you created your brand strategy and what does it look like?

23. Can you use your online business to expand your brick and mortar store?

24. Is there value to having both an online and offline store?

25. Does your website accurately reflect your vision, goals or agenda?

26. Does social media play a part in your current marketing plan?

27. What social media do you now use and what social media can you add to your marketing mix?

28. What percentage of your business makes a profit either online or offline?

29. Who do you employ that makes your business attractive or great?

DEFINE YOUR EXPERIENCE AND LEADERSHIP QUALITIES

1. What is your experience in your field or industry?

2. What is your education level and how can you bring it up to date, if necessary?

3. How often do you upgrade your knowledge of your field or industry?

4. On a scale of one to ten, how would you rate your passion for your position or business?

5. What good leadership qualities do you have and how do they affect your success?

DEFINE YOUR IDEAL CUSTOMER

1. Who specifically is your current ideal customer?

2. What customer would you rather reach?

3. What is customer's pain point or what is keeping them up at night?

4. What are you doing now to reach customers and solve their problem?

5. What are you doing to keep the customers you have?

6. What are their demographics?
      Age?
      Gender?
      Race?
      Marital status?
      Family size?

7. What is the area of the country/world where they live?

8. What is their yearly salary?

9. Do they have children or pets?

10. What are they looking for in the way of products or services or content?

11. What are their hobbies or interests?

12. What are their travel desires?

Define Your Competition

1. Who is your local competition?

2. Name five competitors in your community?

3. How are they different from your business?

4. What business model are they using?

5. Are they your community leaders?

6. What makes them unique?

7. What percentage of sales do they own?

8. In which part of your community are they located?

9. What are they doing to attract customers?

10. What does their branding look like?

11. What specific products or services help them to excel?

12. How did they become #1, #2 or #3?

13. What are their strengths?

14. What are their weaknesses?

15. Who do they employ that makes them unique/great?

What is your Marketing Mix?

Your marketing mix is a set of actions that your small business uses to promote your brand or product. The 4 P's are Price, Product, Promotion and Place.

1. What did you do in the past that worked or didn't work?

2. What ideas do you have moving forward?

Badass Important Tip #2: Take the Steps!
Did you fill out this section? If you did, great! You are at an advantage over most other entrepreneurs. If you just skimmed through this section, go back and answer the questions. It's important to do so. If not, you won't be as successful as you desire. You need those answers to proactively get up to speed with your business. ... to be a *Badass*! You'll use this information throughout the rest of the book for attracting and keeping customers.

* *Growth Hacking for Hair Salons* is meant to be used alongside my book, *"How to Organize Your Marketing Campaign, and Hit the Ground Running."* You will find it on Amazon.com as an eBook. The book was endorsed by Jay Conrad Levinson, creator of the top selling marketing books, *Guerrilla Marketing*. Put this link into your browser: https://amzn.to/2ImDuA3

Expert Online Resource:
BusinessAcademy.com and our affiliate partner, CreativeLive, offer an expert online learning experience to help your business standout from your competition.

Build a Standout Business; Don't Let Your Business Get Lost in the Crowd! by Tara Gentile

Your business should be a beacon for the right people. It should effort lessly connect with the customers and clients who can benefit most from the product or service you have to offer.

Throughout the course, we'll tackle goal-setting, community-building, social media, content marketing, metrics and analysis, sales, and product development. By the end of these 25 powerful lessons, you'll have a complete blueprint for building your stand-out business and leading yourself to the success you dream of. Excellent

recommendations by CreativeLive.
BusinessAcademy may be compensated if you purchase a course.

* Copy this link into your browser: http://shrsl.com/1f87f

USE WHAT YOU LEARNED IN CHAPTER TWO:
KNOW WHERE YOU STAND ;
Getting Up to Speed with Assets and Liabilities
1. Define your business.
2. Define your leadership qualities.
3. Define your ideal customer & demographics.
4. Define your competition.
5. Define your past marketing.
6. Build a standout business!
7. There were 2 *Badass important* sections.
8. Two opportunities for expert online learning experiences.

CHAPTER THREE:

THE ONLINE PHENOMENA
Putting Your Best Face/Voice Forward

Okay, here it is … the number one thing that all *Badass Marketers* need to know. You are not in the business of selling products or services or both. You can read that again if you like, but it's true. You are in the business *of building relationships and solving the problems and pain that keep those people up at night, stressed out or unhappy.* For example, they come to you for solutions to their problems, whether it's coping with a bad hair day, getting their nails to grow long, or what tool to use when they want their hair to look like that FB influencer.

They might even be coming to you if they are lonely. People tend to hang out at their local salon, barber shop or nail salon. Your customers just want to get out of the house, or have a new experience. Some of the things people do are related to loneliness. Their problem is your problem and the more solutions you have, the more likely they are to keep returning to your small business. Whatever it is, you want to be on their radar!

Badass Important Tip #3: You Are in the People Business!
People like to do business with people they know, like and trust. So, in whatever marketing capacity you take on this journey to become a successful business person, you are in the *people business.* If people are

happy with your product, service or content, they will return or tell others what a good *Badass* you are. Whether it's the way you design your web pages, promos or promises, or how you respond to a customer's anger, BS or concerns, that will reflect on your business and your bottom line at some point.

Badass Important Tip #4: People Want an Experience!
Whatever kind of service business you own, the second thing that all *Badass Marketers* need to know is that your customers want to have an *experience.* Consumers have come to expect and demand an experience of some sort. Whether you own a chain of hair salons, skin care, nail or barber shops, or a whoop-de-doo website, you are obligated *to create an atmosphere for buying.*

Your atmosphere should be welcoming, user friendly (there's that word again) or easy to navigate, pleasant, thoughtful or consistent. Make it easy and pleasurable for customers to walk through your door, call you on the phone, get an email reply, navigate your website, or read your blog.

*Smaller businesses can provide the personal touch customers are looking for that large companies can't. People have enough stress in their lives, so give your customers something to smile about.

* I get really frustrated when I'm trying to reach a business to get a problem solved and I get the runaround (voicemail hell) or no solution to my satisfaction. I sometimes vow never to return. You don't want that, do you?

Let's Rock Your Email or (hard copy) Mailing List
"The Money is in the List!" I can't tell you how many times I've heard that phrase. It's almost as popular as a phrase as *"Know Thyself!"* Build your mailing list or email list by using the names, addresses and phone numbers from your raffles, customer files, customer surveys and website

forms. Follow in the footsteps of online businesses that capture email addresses with *an enticing free offer of something they find valuable.*

Expert Online Resource:
BusinessAcademy.com and their affiliate partner, CreativeLive, bring you an expert learning experience for writing magnetic emails.

How to Write the Perfect Email by Justin Kerr

Despite the popularity of messaging tools like Slack, HipChat, and Basecamp, email remains the single most important means of communication in corporate America. And yet, people love to bash email, most likely because they're simply not good at writing them. Being able to write an effective email is a critical skill for anyone wanting to be successful at their job.

Best-selling author Justin Kerr breaks down the do's and don'ts of email writing and how good emails with bullet points hold the secret to an optimal work/life balance. You'll learn how to: win an email fight, get replies to your emails, set effective deadlines, design a quality email, and avoid using attachments. We may be compensated if you purchase a course.

* Copy this link into your browser: http://shrsl.com/1f8m8

Okay, Here We Go With the Growth Hacks
1) When potential customers walk through your door, keep a clipboard at the desk for names and email addresses. You can offer customers a sample or small gift, but it usually isn't necessary because they are already there. It's always a welcome gesture if you do offer some small tidbit. Everyone wants something for free, no matter how small or insignificant it is to you. It just might make their day!

2) Send customers your information or enewsletters about your business services and upcoming promotions. Always keep people on your mailing list for at least a year whether they use your services regularly or not – unless they request to be taken off your list.

Exercise: Name the exact date when you will start building a mailing list or email list.

Create A Badass Website

3) A website is basically an online brochure for you or your business that anyone in the world can access. It will show you or your business in a positive light and have enough information on it to attract your target audience. Customers learn how your business can help them or how they can purchase something that can help them in some way. A website can be a selling tool, an informational tool or a source of entertainment (or all three).

* Use your website wisely or it can become a financial drain.

The elements used on a website are really up to you and your business type.

Typically you'll include:

- The Basics: your logo, an About page, a Contact page (email address, street address, phone number and any social media tags), and pages describing your products and/or services.
- Videos, photos, and commentary are standard.
- Many people offer a blog so they can exchange ideas with their audience. In order for your blog to be successful you need to keep your content fresh and updated. Use SEO (Search Engine Optimization so people can find you on search engines like Google or Bing).
- Keep your colors, images and your brand consistent throughout.
- Keep your website simple – don't overload it with too much information or noise.
- Make it interesting, but showcase the main goal of your business.

- Give enough information to your audience for them to understand what you are selling.
- Share prices if possible or let customers know where to find that information.
- Have a great sales page. Make it impactful and remember your *Call to Action!*
- It needs to be positioned correctly to achieve your financial goals.
- Include a sign up form and a free incentive to entice customers to give their email address.
- Include anything else you want your customers to know: sales, open house, coupons etc.

* Make it easy for you to update your website when necessary.

Expert Online Resource:
BusinessAcademy.com and affiliate partner, CreativeLive, bring you an expert learning experience for creating an impactful business website.

Make Your Website Work for You! by Devin Duncan

Drawing on years of experience as an entrepreneur, Devin will teach you how to design your website for optimal sales and customer interaction. You'll learn the psychology behind online sales, how to monetize your products, and the many types of content that make a website clickable and dynamic.

Devin will also cover easy-to-implement techniques for building customer relationships online. Get the tools to build a website that engages your ideal customers and becomes a major source of revenue and sales. Thumbs up by CreativeLive.

BusinessAcademy may be compensated if you purchase a course.

* Copy this link in your browser: http://shrsl.com/1f8dj

Do You Need a Membership Site?

4) Memberships sites are websites that offer specific and usually specialized content that is not found on your regular website. It's usually premium information. Customers sign up with a username and password in order to enter, and they pay you a monthly fee for the privilege of getting your Badass upgraded information. For you, membership sites offer the benefit of recurring revenue from your fans that trust you to deliver the goods, so to speak. You want your fans and new customers to say *"YES"* to you each month. Satisfied customers always return.

They may pay you anywhere from $10-15 a month or hundreds of dollars a month for your expertise. People are willing to pay for good, reliable expertise in a niche they are passionate about.

So what do you need to provide? Here are some ideas: something to entertain them, educate them, surprise them in some unique way, do something faster, easier or more novel.

Take a moment to think about what your favorite customers talk about? What are they buying? What are your newest products? What offers can you give? Keep providing solutions, good content, entertaining dialogue, content, resources, products and services that are addicting. With a big membership you can *Transform Your Hair Salon Into a Badass Money Machine!* Say *"YES!"*

Examples of What You Can Offer:

Beauty and Fashion Advice: point customers to fashion magazines or Instagram posts. New fashion accessories or ideas from your last conference or educational event.

Health Advice: yoga, meditation, exercises, or weight loss.

Food: recipes, cooking procedures, favorite cookbooks or shortcuts.

Gardening: how to grow plants in pots, and solve specific gardening problems.

Relationships: matching people up, advice for what kind of person to avoid, where to find older partners or gay partners.

The Tip of the Iceberg

The sky is the limit with what you can create. Remember that you have the entire world at your fingertips (no pun intended). As you can see, there are plenty of topics that will do well with a membership site.

- You can expand into webinars, special trainings, coaching and perhaps a retreat or conference.
- Start at a low price (less than $10) in the beginning, then increase the price as your content becomes more valuable.
- Get emails for your list.

Stories are King! Remember to Tell Your Story

5) Mark Zuckerberg (co-founder of FaceBook.com) says, *"Stories are the future."* Use *Stories* on your FaceBook pages; business or personal. The best place to tell your story is on your website, on your *About* page. This is where people look to see who you are, and how you got to where you are. Tell the story of your background, how you got started, who inspired you, what hurdles you had to jump, and how you succeeded in spite of challenges. Make it interesting and personal. Add photos or a video of your business, of you sitting at your reception desk or of your employees doing manicures. Show your awards, trophies and ribbons if you have any. Take your tribe on a tour of your hair salon or barber shop. Make it interesting and fun. Use a series of videos or photos.

My niece in the Midwest is a popular fashion blogger and I often look at her social media posts to see what she is wearing and where she gets her cool clothes. She sometimes includes her family in her photos. There are times when a stiff business photo is acceptable, and other times you want to show bits of your lifestyle and how much fun you're having, like Beth does. Personal photos have a place in your business, and people can relate to who you are, almost as if you are a friend. It's a great relationship building strategy.

Consider having a friend interview you on camera, and you can tell your story that way. Talk about your goals, and what you did to succeed. Show your portfolio or anything fascinating about you or your business. Alternate between close-ups and distance shots. Use an interesting location for variety.

Or if you're not comfortable speaking on video, then just shoot a series of photos of you, your team and your workplace with some interesting facts and dialogue written on the side. Consider doing a voiceover that explains your business. Your fans or tribe want to know who you are and how you apply your creative process. Be a *Badass* and give them what they want!

Expert Online Resource:
BusinessAcademy.com and affiliate partner, CreativeLive, bring you an expert learning experience for effective storytelling.

Storytelling for Business by Jamie Jensen
(Connect with clients on a deeper level through stories)

Award-winning writer and consultant Jamie Jensen will show you how to craft a brand story that's relevant to your business. She'll walk you through the four main types of stories you can use and explain how each one can yield impressive results. In this class, you'll learn how to: figure out when and where to use story in your copy and content. Decide which story to use depending on your needs and goals.

Create characters, objectives and obstacles for your story. Change your story to keep it fresh and interesting. Identify with your customer when telling your story. Take on the role of expert or mentor to convince your reader to buy. BusinessAcademy may be compensated if you purchase a course.
* Copy this link into your browser: http://shrsl.com/1f85o

Webinars – Learn How to Educate and Sell
6) Webinars are like seminars except that they take place online. It's a way of educating your followers with either your best content, new content or *still viable* content you haven't promoted in a while.

The strategy that most online teachers use is to offer a first class for free. It might be for an hour or so, giving your audience a nice snippet of your content. Make it just enough to whet their appetites and leave them wanting more. It's sort of like taking a bite of chocolate cake, but holding off on the whole thing. You give them some good content and then make your offer. Your special offer is, of course, your best material. This is the real (chocolate cake) that will help them feel fulfilled or in your case like they've received the best value. Having some great testimonials from former students will help them to decide *for* you.

For example, many online teachers will send a series of emails to their list offering a *free* video mini-course of the material their students want. The reader will get 3 five-minute (pre-recorded) videos over the course of three days. At the end of the three-day course comes a pitch to attend a free or low cost online seminar. It might be a one-hour course with more impactful material and a small e-workbook (Give your audience some quick and easy wins so they are confident going forward). Help participants get ready for something bigger. During this time you are building trust and a relationship with each person.

That full seminar is a pre-requisite to attending the BIG ONE, which of course is quite expensive (anywhere from $500 and up, to thousands of dollars). The BIG ONE might offer the teacher's best training, group coaching calls or even two tickets to a live weekend seminar in a major U.S. city. Watch some of these teacher's in action. Learn the ropes, then offer your own outstanding program to your list.

Badass Important Tip #5: Determine the Customers Transformation!
Establish your goal before offering your courses, seminar or challenge. What is the transformation? What is the goal your customers want to reach through your webinar? Will you help them reach it, and how?

* Remember that *trust* is the most important factor when asking for big money from your audience. If they don't trust you to deliver the goods

or give them something they don't already know, then you may not get their money either.

Your Webinar Launch Strategy

1. Start with a *thank you!* Tell them who you are and why you are the one to offer this unique and valuable information.

2. Set expectations with the great content you will offer.

3. Ask, *"What prompted you to schedule this call?"* Find out what inspired listeners, so you can use that information to attract people to your next webinar.

4. Listen carefully to what they say. There might be some gems in there.

5. Thank people for sharing their thoughts.

6. What's included in the package? People who attend weekend seminars are the ones who know you, who have established a relationship with you or trust your reputation.

7. What questions do you have?

8. Overcome objections by showing value.

9. Highlight before and after scenarios, and success stories.

10. Show case studies, if possible.

When Customers Have Price Issues

"I don't have the money!" When people don't buy your webinar, product or service it's not always about price. Sometimes it is, but mostly it's because the have some fear that you will not deliver the goods, or they don't think they can execute your plan (they don't trust themselves), or they don't see the value in what you are offering or how you are offering it. You must (beyond the shadow of a doubt) explain how they are the winner when they purchase (anything from you). A *money back guarantee* is a great incentive for people to at least try it.

People who say they don't have the money often have the money for the things they really care about. How will you convince customers to care about your offering? Is it something that could change his/her life for the better? Testimonials from happy customers are proof.

Get Seen and Heard for FREE. Growth Hacks for Exposure

Get as much exposure as you can:

7) Strike up conversations with people wherever you are. Tell them what you do. Be engaging!

8) Post on every social media platform that has your audience captive.

9) Offer to write a blog post for other sites. We'll talk more about this later.

10) Do a podcast. We'll talk more about this later.

11) Be a guest presenter at local venues or on podcasts.

12) Speak at Cosmetology conferences or other people's events.

13) Write a freelance article and submit it to industry magazines.

14) Co-host a webinar, even if it's for free. Just get your name out there.

15) Appear in someone else's YouTube video. Who do you know?

Resources:

If you have a large audience attending your webinar, it's best to find a platform that can handle your audience so it doesn't crash your computer. Some popular platforms to hold a webinar are with Zoom, FaceBook Live, webinarjam, and GotoMeeting. You can also use Skype for a smaller group. There may be other options in the future.

Create or Join an Online Challenge

16) You can encourage a Community *Challenge* for your niche audience. If you've never participated in a *challenge*, then you are in for a real learning treat. A *challenge* is a competition with yourself, not particularly with another person. You are being challenged to do something that makes your own life better: lose weight, get fit, cook more healthy foods. Choose whatever your customers are drawn to.

Remember the Ice Bucket Challenge?

Oh Yeah! People enjoy the challenge of doing something newsworthy, outrageous and fun. In 2014, celebrities, sports figures and everyday Americans joined in on the *Ice Bucket Challenge* and earned $115 million to raise awareness and donations for the disease ALS (Lou Gehrig's Disease).

Many of us have a need to explore what is possible by losing weight, stopping smoking, running a marathon, climbing the highest mountain or eating the most hotdogs. *The Guinness Book of World Records* is a great example of how people succeed at stretching their capabilities. There are many creative ways to challenge oneself without entering a triathlon, a marathon or a high speed auto race.

I've participated in several challenges and they were all for writers/artists. For example, the first was a *30 Day Online Book Challenge for Writers.* We spent 30 days learning how to write and market our books on various platforms; from blogging to online book tours to using social media. Thirty experienced writing teachers shared their expertise, and challenged us to use their instructions.

My second challenge was a *30 Day Book Series Challenge,* where writers created a new book or used a current one and made a series out of it. The goal was to have at least three books that would sell more copies than one. It would keep the momentum going for readers.

Then there was the *NaNoWriMo* Challenge. That's the *National Novel Writing Month Challenge* that challenges you to write a 50,000 word novel in one month … November. I made it to 35,000 words on my first try in 2018. I won my second try in 2019 with nearly 51,000 words in 30 days.

Urban Sketchers has an artist challenge where members try to sketch 100 people in one week. I made it to 85 sketches. Whether you reach the goal or not, challenges are fun and worthwhile. And yes, they are meant to challenge you, and take you to a higher level in your craft.

Challenges often cost money to participate, which means they have the potential to be lucrative. If you create one, realize that these events can be a lot of work, and you may want to hire other experts to contribute their expertise rather than doing it all yourself. You can interview the experts in advance and play the recordings online. You can also pre-record some audios or videos, and do some live. It depends on your topic and the depth you want to go into. If you want to have a Q&A, then your webinar should be live. Some challenges are free (by donation) and others cost around $100 or so. Check with the organizer. As a sidenote, it may not be worth it if you don't have a lot of followers, or it may become a way to get more followers.

Question: What kind of a challenge could your salon facilitate?

PODCASTING

17) As opposed to video, a podcast is basically an audio delivery mechanism or a medium by which you can share audio content online (your website, blog or iTunes). It's like having your own radio station. What could be better than that? Subscribers download your Badass content/messages to listen at their convenience. They may listen on their computer, tablet, cell phone or while walking on a treadmill. It's a popular way to get your message out to listeners.

Many people like the option of *listening* as opposed to reading. This medium is also great for long distance drivers or people who are visually impaired, sitting in traffic or perhaps busy with mind-less tasks. People listen to podcasts on their computer while they're creating art or cleaning their office. Talk about products that have helped your customers or interview happy customers.

Potential clients can download your content and listen to your advice or knowledge on a specific topic that interests them. There are endless topics you could use, but your best choice is something you are passionate about and relates to your business. It could be a talk around beauty treatments, skin allergies, trendy nail polish colors or fashion.

The keys to effective podcasting are:
1. Spend time perfecting your script. Have a plan before you record it. Use stories to get listeners' attention. Make each show about the same amount of time … 20-30 minutes or less.
2. Record someone with a powerful voice to announce you.

Interviewing knowledgeable people makes the podcast more interesting for listeners. Get to the point quickly. You can do a wrap-up at the end, driving home important points to remember.

3. Use your best information and remember to edit what you recorded, making your material sound more professional.

4. Make it entertaining. Get comfortable with speaking, and don't worry about your voice. Add background music that starts out loud and lower the sound while you speak. You could license a track from an independent musician or use a clip of royalty free music.

5. Include testimonials; *"And here's what Mary Smith said about ... (your product or service)."*

6. Share contact information like your blog, website or email address.

7. List your podcast with *iTunes*.

How to Get Started in Podcasting

18) You can spend a lot of money on expensive equipment, but to get started all you need is a headset and a microphone. You can go to the Audible.com website (free recording software) and create an audiophile or if you have a Mac computer you can use the pre-installed *Garageband* to record your voice. My iMac has a built in microphone and it's very good and clear.

19) Some types of video will enable you to export the audio portion so you can re-use them as podcasts. This is a great way to recycle information you've already recorded.

Exercise: Which of your videos on YouTube can be exported to audio?

20) In Chapter Two *"Know Where You Stand"* you explored your competition. Now is the time to use that information. What are other podcasters in your industry talking about? What is the quality of their podcasts and how can you offer a better experience?

- Is there someone interesting you can interview?
- Can you offer quotes and/or a review of someone else's lecture?
- Do research on your topic and find some interesting facts.
- Be a resource for people who wants tips, facts and figures.

Exercise: Who else is recording podcasts on your topic and how can you do it better?

Expert Online Resource:
BusinessAcademy.com and affiliate partner, CreativeLive, bring you an expert learning experience about broadcasting your expertise.

Turn Your Expertise into a Podcast by Cal Peternell and Christina Loring

If you're an expert on a certain topic, you probably have a lot of great fodder for a podcast. But how do you transform your vast knowledge and expertise into something that will engage listeners and keep them coming back for more? Sound-oriented storyteller, creator, and producer Christina Loring and chef/cookbook author Cal Peternell will show you how to take your raw material and create an audio narrative that's compelling and seamless.

They'll help you get comfortable with the podcasting format and establish the methods and collaborations that are essential to your success. You'll learn how to integrate instructions and teachings in an engaging way and much more. There are a variety of podcast courses on the www.businessacademy.com blog. BusinessAcademy may be compensated if you purchase a course.

* Copy this link into your browser: http://shrsl.com/1f8rh

CONTENT IS KING!
Badasses Know How to Write Effective Content!
Do you know how to write content for your ads, for your email campaigns, for your posters, books, or press releases? It's time to start learning how to write copy that converts regular consumers into *paying*

customers. Writing engaging content or ads is critical to your success. That's so in traditional marketing as well as social media.

Create Content for Social Media

21) I'm going to start off by saying the best content you can write is the content you are passionate about. Do it yourself if you have the time and ability. Sure, you can hire someone else to write your content and it might be fine. You can always edit it later to make it more along the lines of what you would say, offering your personal perspective. I would suggest testing out a few content writers to save you some time, and then decide if that's for you.

The best content will understand your customer's problems and come up with a good solution. Or help the customer reach a goal, like growing out their hair to 'all one length.' Here I am building on what I said earlier that it's all about the client. Show how you find short effective solutions to their issues.

What transformation can you offer? Amplify the problem, give it a voice and tell how your solution changed your life or made you look 10 years younger. Or how you helped your current customers to have healther looking fingernails, better skin care or shinier hair.

Expert Online Resource:
BusinessAcademy.com and their affiliate partner, CreativeLive, bring you an expert learning experience in writing valuable and effective content.

How to Create Addictive Content by Melissa Cassera

It's critical that your articles, blog posts, reviews and videos are thoughtfully prepared and offer value. Melissa will show you how to use Hollywood storytelling techniques to create content that entices people to read, excites them to share, and moves them to buy.

In this class, you'll learn how to: Understand your audience and the content they crave. Repurpose each piece of content for maximum exposure. Avoid creating boring or corporate content. Uncover your unique voice and style. Create a thriving content-creation process. Write sizzling headlines and effective calls to action. Leverage user-generated content for added credibility. Business Academy may be compensated if you purchase a course.

* Copy this link into your browser: http://shrsl.com/1f91b

---

22) Sometimes your ideal client wants to read a book or watch a video, and other times they just want a simple checklist. Offering all three should keep everyone happy. Offer valuable information that will make your customer's life better. How about a checklist for every customer regarding how to take care of their skin between visits.

Remember that people buy from an emotional standpoint, not always a logical one!
You can direct your ideal client to your blog where you've already included critical information that they are searching for. How do you know that? You did your research, and know that teenagers need certain information or new people in town need a checklist of personal services to check off. There is an endless array of questions where people need answers.

Testimonials, Referrals and Reviews
23) Include testimonials, referrals or reviews if you have some, either written or in video format. I attended a live seminar by a popular speaker, and during the seminar guests were invited to stay afterward and offer a video testimonial. There was a long line of fans waiting to be on video to give kudos to the speaker. This is a great FREE *growth hacking* opportunity.

Do you have regular customers who come to your hair salon, skin care center, nail salon, boutique or spa? Ask if they'd like to offer a video testimonial. People like to see themselves on camera (blog, website, in store) and are willing to give a *kind word* for a business they like. Get every testimonial you can get your hands on, even if it's written. Use the excellent testimonials or referrals everywhere you can. Use them in all your print and online media: ads, web site, brochures, Facebook page, ebooks and books.

* Always include a call to action! It's important that every bit of your marketing materials *ask for the sale!*

24) Public Domain Content

This is an area to use if you are interested in writing about your industry. You can access public domain content and change the wording etc. to make it your own. You may find information that you can use. This is content (books, articles, comics, and pamphlets etc. from the U.S. government or private sources) where the copyright has run out, and it is okay for you to buy it, use it and re-sell it. Sometimes public domain content is free and sometimes you pay. Find public domain content via your favorite search engine.

25) Articles and EBooks for Sale

You can also buy content from a writer in a specific niche. He or she is a ghost writer and writes with the intention to sell their works to you or anyone else who is interested in their topic: beauty, fashion, business etc. They expect that you might modify the material to be what you like, and that's perfectly fine. You can look online for *public domain books, articles or pamphlets.*

26) Micro-content

This is content that is short, to the point, and easy to produce and consume. You might create small pieces of informational content. For example: find a quote that you find meaningful that also has something to do with your business. Write a brief paragraph about it stating your perspective and then post it on your blog, or social media platforms (if appropriate).

Choose your topic and give 3-5 tips. Post 3 times a day if you have the time. You can use it on all the social media platforms including Pinterest.com (include an image, a link and a call to action). I'll talk later about info-graphics and how to create them.

27) Book Reviews

On my former business blog I wrote book reviews of new books that I liked. I would write a brief critique, then put my own spin on the topic. It was an easy way of creating interesting content that my audience enjoyed. Go to Amazon and choose books in your field (beauty business).

Resource:

You can find out what people are looking for on social media or what's trending by typing (into Google) keywords or keywordseverywhere. This will give you more options for content.

28) Batch Your Content

What I discovered is that a lot of experts and business owners who create content *batch their content*. Do it once and drip the content out over time. By that I mean if you use video or photography in your marketing, take a lot of your photos or videos in one day. Edit them, then spread them out over the month by using them on your blog, website, YouTube videos or other social media platforms. It saves time and energy because you've spent one day on work that you can distribute over time. Photograph your favorite hairstyles.

* If you are a fashion blogger doing a photography shoot, you may want to bring a variety of clothes and shoes to change into so it doesn't look like you have only one outfit.

29) Recycle Your Content

Here are some great hints for getting more mileage out of your content. Write a book, then take small sections out of the book and give them a different spin. I turn those snippets into my blog content or a checklist. I put them into my emails. When I have enough blog content I turn it into an eBook. I may write a short eBook on a specific topic, then fit it into another book (as a chapter) with similar content.

There are many ways to recycle your content and use it again and again. How about making an online video course out of a book you wrote, or even an audio book?

30) Use other peoples content – Yes, you can repost, retweet and resend/share

Find content from other pages on the internet or social media platforms. Content = photos, videos, music, articles, recipes, quotes.

Build a fan base of customers who want what you have to offer. Give first to get.

- Think about customers, and see if they like your content. Try it out. You are doing this for them.
- What do you think your fans will enjoy? Test it to see if other ads work.
- Sign in on your FB page, go to your home page and search your news feed. Start *liking* other people's FB posts, those who relate to or compliment yours and get content from them. Share that on your newsfeed. Most of us have friends who recycle fun or interesting videos, photos etc. There is a never-ending supply of material on FB.
- The better idea is to join FB, or LinkedIn groups of like-minded people who may also supply you with good options for content.

* Beware that you are not plagiarizing another person's work. Always ask permission.

31) Earn Passive Income (Affiliate Marketing)

Affiliate marketing is a another good way to earn passive income. An affiliate partner is a business collaborator that has a product or service that you like and want to offer to your audience. For various reasons, you may not have the capability or capacity to create their product or service. The products/services should be along the line of what you are already selling, but is uniquely different.

That business did all the work: research, manufacturing, marketing and outreach etc. You make a deal to sell their product on your website or in your store, and they typically give you the their links, product knowledge and special sales. You make a monthly commission or fee on your sales. We call it passive income.

For example, for passive income you might be selling fashion jewelry or handbags out of your hair or nail salons and on your website. A handmade jewelry maker might come by and offer their unique items, and someone else offers their handbags or wallets. They get exposure in your salon and you make money on what you sell. You promote all of your fashion products in your salon, and on your website.

Typically, affiliate marketing is done on websites. Various other online companies want additional exposure, and are willing to pay you a commission for your effort. That's how BusinessAcademy.com is set up. I found that enrolling local businesspeople to create their own online courses turned out to be a slow process, so I found several companies that wanted to market their product to my exact audience. Here is the process for *Affiliate Marketing* and *Earning Passive Income*:

1. Research affiliate marketing companies or local handcrafters.
2. Choose and sign up with companies that have complementary products worth your attention.
3. Experience and test products for yourself/quality control.
4. Add links and promotional information on your website or blog.
5. You must say in your marketing that *you receive a commission on your affiliate's products*.
6. Promote your affiliate in your email blasts or programs. Include links in your emails.

7.   Receive your commissions from your affiliates.

* **Resource:** I use an affiliate marketing company called <u>www.shareasale.com</u> where you can find a number of companies who offer passive income marketing.

Avoid Marketing Fear

Many new small business owners and entrepreneurs are already in fear about what needs to be done to increase traffic, how to do it, and avoid mistakes. Are you afraid of losing money, and not getting the results you want? It's normal to have some fear around marketing your business in a new way, especially when limited financial resources are at risk. I know what that's like ... been there, done that! Do everything you can to limit your risks. That's what *growth hacking* is about, choosing cost effective promotions to grow and build your business.

Everyone has to start somewhere. You will have more success if you just take *baby steps* toward your goals. Don't try to do everything all at once. Do your research in Chapter Two. You're going to get a lot of ideas in this book, so do your best to strategically reach your target audience.

Treat these growth hacks like they're on a buffet, choose what you like and leave the rest. Learn either strategically or through trial and error how to get your small business noticed and still make a profit. I'll talk about *testing* your ads in the coming chapters, and that should alleviate some of your fears.

USE WHAT YOU LEARNED IN CHAPTER THREE

THE ONLINE PHENOMENA;
Putting Your Best Face/Voice Forward
1. Build relationships.
2. Know that customers want an experience.
3. How to rock your email/mailing list.
4. Create a website.
5. Decide on a membership site.
6. Tell your story.
7. Offer webinars.
8. Create or Join a *Challenge* and engage your customers.
9. Offer a podcast if it suits you and you have time.
10. Write content: public domain, micro-content, book reviews, batching and recycling content.
11. There are *thirty one Growth Hacks* in this chapter to help you in your business.
12. Five opportunities for an expert learning experience!

Notes:

Notes:

CHAPTER FOUR:

TARGET SOCIAL MEDIA PLATFORMS
Be Where the Action Is

First of all, it's important to know that social media platforms are devised mostly for networking, even more than marketing. That's why people go there ... to connect with other people, and for everyone to have a voice. People use their voices in many ways: to say *"hello!"* give advice, share what's going on in their lives, express their opinions, and talk about what they have to offer that may help others.

The last reason is why your salon or skin care business will be using social media to reach the masses: *your offer to help others*. This section is about those social platforms ... the people who use them and how you may capture their attention and possibly some of their disposable income. The key idea here is to *create value with your product or service* ... otherwise you may be ignored!

PART ONE: Social Media Marketing and Networking; How to Be a Badass!

Using social media as a platform for promoting your business products or services is built on the term *social* as in *socializing*. That's what people are doing there: sharing their voices, opinions and perceptions. Each platform is built to attract a certain part of the population, dependent on certain demographics: age, gender, education, personal interests etc. Some platforms will attract more than one demographic. We'll talk more about that later.

These social platforms are free to participate, so anyone and everyone can join in and be a part of the conversation. Because there are so many people socializing, the owners of the various platforms (Facebook, Pinterest etc.) have developed a way to earn money from their captive audience and that's called advertising. These platforms attract a huge audience with needs and desires. The goal (for the *Badass Marketer*, YOU) is to provide solutions for those needs and desires via your paid advertisements.

Technically it's brilliant: online worldwide platforms are provided by technology giants for every kind of person to hang out, meet other people who are like-minded, share personal interests, ideas and creativity. What a great and innovative world, and life changing idea!

Businesses like yours provide solutions or entertainment for the masses and the platform owners (FB) make tons of money for offering advertising space. The idea is that you, the business owner providing solutions or entertainment, also make money. But it gets tricky because there is a learning curve to selling online products and services. There are rules of the highway, so to speak. Since it's a social platform based on connections and free information, you need to provide your own brand of content in order to participate and be successful.

You offer your info for free to attract attention and/or you create advertising that you pay for in order to attract consumers' money. The challenge is in creating the right offer, an offer that attracts your ideal client (the one you wrote about in Chapter Two) and gets them to your door or your website. That's called the *Marketing Mix*, that I mentioned in an earlier chapter. You are offering the right product to the right customer at the right price and in the right place. Sure, people will click on your ads to learn more, and possibly buy stuff. That's Face-Book's strategy for attracting advertising income, entertainment and engagement.

Why is Social Media Marketing Rocket Science, and How Do You Harness it?

This information is for those of you who do not know how social media marketing works or how to use *growth hacking* as the rocket ship for the growth of your business. Navigating *the Internet Super Highway* can seem like rocket science, and I'm here to tell you that it is. It's complicated, and new tools, software, apps and systems or *Rocket Fuel* turn up on a daily basis. Mix *growth hacking* in with the traditional marketing methods that have been around almost forever and it gets tricky. Resources are available to help you through the online jungle. You'll find many of them in these chapters.

You can't transform your hair salon into a *Badass Money Machine* if you don't keep up with trends and technology. It's just a part of doing business, and it's actually not difficult once you either learn how to do it on your own, or find someone (a cost efficient online teacher) to guide you. You also have the option of paying a tech person to do it for you, but then that's not very cost efficient … not a *growth hack*.

Get Your Social Media Education

There are many options for learning how to navigate social media platforms: online courses, live courses, books or YouTube videos. The value in online courses is that you can learn anything and everything in your spare time, and at a reasonable price. You do have to put in the time, take action and know that in the long run, it's time and money well spent. You can learn how to look at analytics and metrics (behind the scenes), and see what's working and what isn't. *Badass* independent entrepreneurs can quickly learn how to update a website or blog in a matter of minutes without having to hire someone every single time something needs to be done. Learning to do these updates for your self is more cost effective in the long run.

Badass Important Tip # 4: Put in the Time!

I'm going to cover some basic and not so basic material for start up business owners like yourself. There are many thick books written on the different aspects of social media marketing. It's beyond the scope of this book to teach you everything you need to know, especially when new updates are happening on a daily basis.

You can still be a *Badass* with social media, but you have to put in the time to learn. Throughout this section I will suggest free or low cost online courses in social media marketing that can help you learn the details, make less mistakes, and get more mileage from your advertising budget.

Determine Your Budget

Promote your business with a monthly advertising budget. Determine how much you can spend each month. The *U.S. Small Business Administration* recommends spending 7-8% of your gross revenue for advertising and marketing. Don't use up the entirety of your advertising budget right away. Allocate it in batches. And use this important tip: Test everything, especially before you start spending your money. You can start with as little as $1-5 in the platforms' ad manager.

Badass Important #5: Be Mindful of Privacy Concerns

Keep in mind that the Internet and social networks are not private. Anytime you sign up for anything online you are being tracked. Your information is often shared or sold to third parties. Your purchase history is shared across platforms. I use the Internet to order printing or purchase equipment, and for weeks I am barraged by advertising from those companies through my email and online platforms. Keep in mind there is no privacy when you use social media or the Internet. Your business is everyone's business.

Reuse Your Assets and Liabilities

In Chapter Two you identified every detail about your business: what your business is selling, your ideal customer, and your competition. You'll use all that same information when you market your nail or hair salon on social media. You are still building relationships and engagement, like you do with traditional media, but it's more personal and on many more platforms.

Ask yourself some additional questions using the information you already know. I'll reiterate that information here:
1. Who is your ideal client? Seniors, children, men?
2. What is the niche you want to attract? Young women 21-40 yrs. old
3. What value are you offering? Lower prices, more experience.
4. What problems are you solving? Hair color, curly hair, nail diseases, facial hair?
5. What one, two or three platforms will reach your ideal customer?
6. What are the *keywords* that people are searching for?

PART TWO: KEEPING TRACK OF YOUR PROMOTIONS
Utilize Your Marketing Calendar
Set up a *Marketing Calendar* where you can plan and see all the promotions you intend to have for each month. It's best to have a consistent number of promotions each month. It's important to be consistent in your style: look, feel, content etc., of your materials and decorations. Stay consistent within your brand's image.

Exercise: Buy a large wall calendar (for the year) at an office supply store and write in all the promotions (Social Media and/or Traditional) that you intend to do this year. It'll help you keep track of your yearly marketing campaign and what needs to be done in advance.

PART THREE: What are the Most Important Social Media Platforms ... The Big Seven!

The Big Seven Social Media Platforms that you may want to be a part of: Facebook.com, Instagram.com, LinkedIn, Pinterest.com, Snapchat. com, Twitter.com, and YouTube.com.

I'm going to write about each one of these platforms, and give you the most pertinent information so you can choose which platforms to include in your social media marketing plan. After I give you the run-down of who is out there, I'll give you some more information that is important to know in developing your strategy for your *Badass Money Machine*.

Expert Online Resource:
BusinessAcademy.com and affiliate partner, CreativeLive, offer an online learning experience for social media domination!

_____

Build a Social Media Plan That Actually Makes Money
by Ryan Deiss

We're constantly being told how social media marketing is essential to reaching customers and driving sales. What's sorely missing is a clear guide about how to ensure your social media marketing efforts aren't just wasting time but advancing your business objectives.

You'll learn how to: identify the real goals of social media marketing, cut through the clutter and engage with your ideal customer, figure out which channels are worth your time and which ones you can ignore, audit your profiles and those of your competition, create content that's unique and catchy, understand which metrics matter and so much more. Highly recommended by CreativeLive. BusinessAcademy may be compensated if you purchase a course.

* Copy this link into your browser: http://shrsl.com/1f8qn

_____

* These Social Media Platforms are arranged in alphabetical order!

FACEBOOK

Facebook is one of the most popular social media platforms. It's free to use, and easy to set up a personal page and a business page. Face-Book makes their money by selling advertising. For regular users, advertisements show up in their newsfeed as well as in a sidebar. FB tracks their *likes*, profile and general information so they can target them to advertisers who have paid to get in front of them, and that's you and your hair, skin, nail or spa business.

For instance, I belong to a Meetup group called *Urban Sketchers* and members post their art on FB so we can see each other's creative efforts. FB sees my interests and then targets me for classes in drawing, sketching or painting. Business owners (like you) who advertise on FB are betting that a certain amount of people will decide to buy.

For example, if you post personal information regarding your religion, political views, business interests or personal interests, FB will cater to your likes, and show you information that will appeal to you.

By the same token, if you have a barber shop and decide to advertise on FB, your ads will show up on the newsfeed or side bar of people who have a history of buying barbering services. Where it shows up and how often depends on your budget. You want to pay for *targeted ads*. That's why it's important to know who your ideal client is, what their interests are, their location and what social media platform they use for services.

* *The more you know about your customer allows you to target them more effectively.*

1) If you want to reach people in a certain demographic (your home town or city) or area of personal interest, find the platform where they hang out. If you want to learn about and be successful with FB advertising, study the advertising that shows up in your own newsfeed or sidebar. It's specific to you so it should be useful for your purposes. Are they using video or a photo with links? Click on the link and see what's offered. If you find it of value, you could sign up and see how

many people choose to spend their money or not. You can learn a lot from the examples of other advertisers.

Who Hangs Out On Facebook?
Facebook is the largest social media company, with two billion users and counting. It's best for reaching the millennial generation and Gen X as well as an older population.

Facebook Groups
Starting your own FB group is an excellent way to build a community of like-minded people. Your group can be open to everyone or a closed group, where people must follow specific rules and fans must post/comment on certain topics. You can either start a FB group or join one. It's a great platform to find details about your target market. You can ask questions, congratulate them or simply discover what they are interested in knowing, doing, being or having.

What are Customers Doing on Facebook?
Most people use FB as a way of sharing their voices on most any topic of interest, as well as photos, videos and general commentary. It's a way of staying in touch with friends and family who may live elsewhere in the country or the world. People use FB to promote causes and share their creativity. They also use it to learn about local and worldwide events. Its uses are limitless.

According to my research, if you want to reach an older population (40+) FaceBook is the platform you want to target for new business.

How Can You Promote Your Business and Sell Retail on FaceBook?
In her online course "What You Need to Sell on *Social Media, A Complete Guide,*" Mei Pak talks about selling retail items on Facebook. She specializes in physical products made by *Makers, Artists and Designers.* Mei says for your sales to be the best, offer special sales when your fans are most engaged on FB. Pay special attention to time zones

if your customers are from other countries.

2) Start a Facebook business page so your fans will return to either see your new products or interact with you and other customers. Here is a short checklist of important things to remember when using FB for advertising:

- Show your ads on the desktop and newsfeed, (not on side of page) to save money.
- Always be testing and optimizing.
- Create an ad, make a copy, and tweak one small thing (your title or something) and go back to look at your analytics to see what worked. Test everything so you don't waste your money.
- Post your FB page in as many places as you can.
- Send an email to your customer list, asking if they have seen your FB business page yet?
- Send a pitch to influencers who have a larger audience. Ask if they are interested in collaborating with you.
- Post great content for your fans, always teaching them something new. Remember that your posts show up in your fans' and friends' newsfeed, allowing you free advertising. That's a *hack!*
- Testing an ad or book cover? Post your ad or questions on your newsfeed for good, free feedback. Another *hack!*

3) To build engagement, build a photo content library of you, your products, projects, your staff and *behind the scenes* shots. This will heighten interest with new customers. Remember when we talked about telling your story? This is another opportunity to expand on that.

I also encouraged you to batch your information. This is another good time to do that, with your retail projects. Write all your content, organize photos and set up a plan to drip information over a period of time.

Another thing to batch is other people's content. Find photos, articles, quotes, videos and other interesting content to share online.

Pinterest.com is a good place to find helpful content.

4) Build Community with Your Tribe on FB

If possible, respond to all comments on your FB page within 12-24 hours. A quick response time may help your fans feel like you care about them, and are there for them. People want to feel special, like they matter. So build that relationship if you want return visits and sales. When it comes to product sales, people like to see good quality photos, so make the time and energy to showcase them.

5) Facebook Messenger

The *Messenger* function is good for a mini-chat ... meeting someone on a FB group who you might want to interact with in private (aside from the group listening in to your conversation). It's a great way to make a more personal connection with someone you may want to do business with. Use it to build trust, generate leads, and set appointments.

Exercise: What are your first thoughts on how you can access Facebook for your business?

Expert Online Resource:
BusinessAcademy.com and its affiliate partner, CreativeLive, offer this expert online learning experience to upgrade your FaceBook marketing skills.

Turn Clicks Into Customers on FaceBook by Billy Gene

Billy Gene, one of the top online marketing influencers in the world, will help you create a video script that turns strangers into customers on Facebook without spending a single penny.

You'll learn how to: attract customers organically, create entertaining content that compels people to click, gather the tools you need to film your own video, write a successful video script, including webinars, sales letters and demonstrations, evoke emotion and anticipation among your viewers. BusinessAcademy may be compensated if you purchase a course.

* Copy this link in your browser: http://shrsl.com/1f8q7

INSTAGRAM

Instagram is the up and comer, and the fastest growing social media platform. Instagram is a photo and video-sharing social networking service owned by FaceBook. It was launched in 2010.

Who Hangs Out on Instagram?

Young professionals and people who are interested in following the activities of people/celebrities they like.

What are They Doing?

People are taking photos, recording video, gaining followers or using it for business.

How Can You Promote Your Business and Make Money on Instagram?

6) Focus on video to get the best engagement. Tell your story through video, photos and interesting content/quotes etc. Also, read my content on creating videos (YouTube section, this chapter). Instagram stories – you can create an ad for this area.

Visibility on Instagram

The downside: if you posted an advertisement 2-3 days ago, you go lower in visibility. You never see 100% of posts.

7) How to Make Retail Sales on Instagram

- Make a list of hashtags that you think people will want to use.
- Make it a habit to respond to customers who request information.
- Choose the right hashtags – what are they posting about?
- Know your ideal customer, what hashtags are they using?

- Go into Instagram to find your ideal customer.
- Post once a day. Instagram is more low maintenance than other social media sites.

Make it clear that you have a viable business when someone visits your page. They'll understand that products are available for purchase. Customers want to see product photos, lifestyle photos, and photos of your salon/studio/shop or spa. You can even offer a short video of you or an employee taking customers through your business location.

Expert Online Resource:
BusinessAcademy.com and its affiliate partner, CreativeLive, offers an Instagram online course to help you navigate this popular social platform

Hype Your Brand on Instagram by Sue B. Zimmerman

Instagram is one of the fastest-growing social marketing platforms for business. Sue will explore every aspect of the Instagram universe— from how to use Instagram Stories and Highlights to how to master the site's elusive algorithm — so you're ready and able to grow your presence, build and engage your audience, and rack up sales. BIG thumbs Up from CreativeLive! BusinessAcademy may be compensated if you purchase a course.

* Copy this link into your browser: http://shrsl.com/1f8py

Exercise: What are your first thoughts on how you can access Instagram for your business?

LINKEDIN

Who Hangs Out on LinkedIn?

LinkedIn is a social media platform for large and small business owners, entrepreneurs and corporate employees. Users tend to be in a higher income bracket. LinkedIn is a good place to go if you or your company is looking to reach out Generation X'ers. These are people born between 1965 and 1980. As of this writing, they are between 45-55 years old. There are 82 million Gen X'ers in the U. S.

What are People Doing on LinkedIn?

This primarily business platform is for people who are making business connections and professional referrals. As a member you may find a job or make a connection with someone who can help you get a job. As a business owner you may offer vacant positions.

Joining LinkedIn has many benefits. You can promote your business or look for businesses who may have products or services you can use (vendors). Members connect with other members for networking and sharing business tips and ideas.

Quality content is consistent on this platform. It's a good platform for getting a conversation going about a business-related topic. Posts and articles are often about personal and business growth and how to reach your goals.

A LinkedIn member can also post comments or content on the LinkedIn platform, another way of attracting attention and helping other connections with your expertise or support.

How Does LinkedIn Work?

Anyone can join on LinkedIn with a user name and password, and set up a profile/resume. People will see your profile and ask to be connected with you. You have the option of connecting with that person or not. LinkedIn will send you an email message asking if you want to connect with that company or person. It's the same sort of thing that Facebook does, where people ask to be friends and you agree to accept that person or not. When I first joined I considered it an opportunity to build up my business contacts, so I accepted everyone's invitation to be a *connection*. Some people say not to do that, but I personally don't see any harm it, but you should do whatever you feel comfortable with.

How Can You Promote Your Business and Make Money on LinkedIn? It's really all about making the right connections. If you sell certain products like jewelry, handbags or only beauty products, you may seek to find retail outlets for your business, or even manufacturers. Or perhaps information is more of what you are seeking, such as someone who knows of a good manufacturing plant in China or India or elsewhere in the world, especially if you want to have a private label.

Whole books are written on this subject and it is beyond the scope of this book to offer that level of advice. In the resource section you will find my recommendations.

Expert Online Resource:
BusinessAcademy.com and affiliate partner, CreativeLive, offer an online course to give you more in-depth knowledge of LinkedIn

---

Reach All-Star Status on LinkedIn by Marcus Murphy

Learn how to fully leverage LinkedIn and it's many features to achieve your business and career goals. Marcus will offer an in-depth guide to getting the most out of LinkedIn, including attracting quality prospects, amassing a valuable network, and growing your personal brand and more. BusinessAcademy may be compensated if you purchase a course.

* Copy this link into your browser: http://shrsl.com/1f8q4
Exercise: What are your first thoughts on how you can access LinkedIn for your business?

PINTEREST

Some people think of Pinterest as a social scrapbooking site. It's actually a digital pin up board. Two billion people search for things on Pinterest every single month. It's great for ecommerce (lots of visually oriented consumer content). Pinterest helps people discover what they like or love and plan to buy. You might consider it to be a visual discovery search engine or even a digital catalog.

Who Hangs Out on Pinterest?

30+ something females, but also many men. There are an estimated 70% Female and 30% male visitors each month. Many young mothers and young professionals use Pinterest to create their own boards and shop through other Pinner's boards.

What are People Doing on Pinterest?

They are people who are interested in making their lives better. To get started, you need to sign up (like most social media sites) and you are asked what you are interested in. Pinterest will set up a board and pull from all the places that offer what you ask for: recipes, clothes, shoes, travel, home décor, weight loss tips, children's items etc.
* *Pinterest is focused on ecommerce and is retail oriented.*

People are looking for interesting content (hobbies), offering content, finding solutions to problems (hairstyles, skin care, weight etc.)

How Does Pinterest Work?

The people that hang out on Pinterest create what they call *boards* where they pin visual items, almost like a bulletin board. You will find recipes, easier ways to do things (tips), fashion, cosmetics, children's clothes or really just about anything. Pin photos and text of your products and include a small list of the benefits of buying your shampoo, brushes, unique nail polishes, or fashion line. If you are also an author you can pin your book covers, characters, photos of you or your writing area.

8) Stay engaged in the conversation. Posting your content is good, but *better* is reciprocating by re-pinning content, liking other's pins and commenting on other boards. One must be proactive. Try following the Pinterest boards of people you like: chefs, fashionista's etc.

How Can You Promote Your Business and Make Money on Pinterest?
9) Sign up for a business account in order to take part in advertising. Make sure the names of your boards have catchy titles and always include a link back to your website, your Amazon sellers page or anyplace that sells your products or services (Shopify, Etsy, Ebay?). Remember that a Pinterest post has a life of about 3.5 months, which is longer than most other social media platforms.

10) First think about what Pinners might be interested in, and if they are your target audience. Then make a plan on what photos and content will draw attention to your brand. If you have many products, you can build a board for each one, designating the benefits that Pinners are looking for.

You'll post your info-graphics, which are a combination of images (pictures or illustrations) and some impactful brief text. Basically, it's valuable content that you believe people on Pinterest might be interested in.

The shape of Info-graphics are typically created to be more long and narrow, almost like a traditional bookmark. You can get great examples of Info-graphics on Google. Just type in 'info-graphics' and many examples will show up. It's a great resource.

To create one, there is usually a prominent headline, an image that is related to what you are promoting, some text (tips, checklist or secrets etc.) and then a link to where you want the reader to go. Ideally this is your website where they can purchase something amazing from you or set up an appointment for your service. You might create some pins with testimonials on them, perhaps with a happy looking customer? There are lots of creative ideas you can implement.

11) One way to get attention is to ask Pinners to contribute information to your board. Let's say you have a new private label skin care line. You could ask Pinners to submit a name, a favorite color or a logo they drew themselves. Do whatever you can to get engagement with your audience. Be creative and give your audience permission to be creative.

How can you help Pinterest Pinners? What expertise do you have that will solve their problems and cause them to come to your business?

- Do you offer webinars, online courses or have a book?
- Weight problem – you have a weight loss clinic, or a spa. You are a fitness coach in your day spa.
- Fashion retailing search problem – Your spa offers yoga clothes, robes and skin care solutions.
- Mens grooming problems – your barber shop helps men create new beard styles and classes on male grooming.
- Body hair problems – you are a waxing Rockstar!

Exercise: What are your first thoughts on how you can access Pinterest for your business?

Expert Online Resource:
www.businessacademy.com **and affiliate partner, CreativeLive, offer an expert online learning experience to make an impact with LinkedIn**

Using Pinterest to Grow Your Business by Alexandra Evjen

Discover how pinning can be one of the best ways to drive sales online. Alexandra Evjen, known as the Pinterest queen, has helped countless brands such as Target, Home Depot and Anthropologie create digital content that keeps consumers wanting more and makes products fly off the shelves. With her creative eye and strategic mind, she'll help you find success on Pinterest too. You'll learn how to: establish your brand, create a powerful, rich and shoppable pin, develop a content strategy for sharing, prep for conversions, understand *Pinterest Analytics* and adjust your game plan based on the data. BusinessAcademy may be compensated if you purchase a course.

* Copy this link into your browser: http://shrsl.com/1f8qh

_____

SNAPCHAT

Snapchat is a popular messaging app that lets users exchange pictures and videos (called snaps) that are meant to disappear after they're viewed. It's advertised as *a new type of camera* because the essential function is to take a picture or video, add filters, lenses or other effects and share them with friends.

Who Hangs Out on Snapchat?

Snapchat.com skews to the very young and is worth getting in early if you have the resources. You must be at least 13 years old to register for Snapchat.

What Are Customers Doing?

These people are mostly tweens and teens hanging out, and having fun with images, videos and stories. It's free to download and free to send photos or messages to each other.

How Does it Work?

Snapchat is a place for throwaway content. After getting an up-to-date version you can use special text and colors, filter and various camera features.

How Can You Promote Your Business and Make Money on Snapchat?

Get excited about the channels that your customers are excited about. I have personally not used Snapchat but according to my research you need to start accumulating followers who will see your stories. You will have a core audience when you send *follow requests* to family, friends and other people you're connected with on other social media platforms (your contacts).

Follow other people (public personalities and influencers) that you come across and they may follow you. You eventually build a platform of followers to help each other become more visible. Your messages go out to a wider audience who may frequent your business offerings.

12) Cross-promotion is a good benefit for all parties (See my cross-promotion hack.) **Note:** you may have to pay for shout-outs from high profile individuals. You can use your other social media accounts to advertise your Snapchat activities.

13) Use unique stories and distinct themes to set yourself apart from other people help you to get noticed. Note the themes I've mentioned in Chapter Six: "Create the Almighty Experience, Attract Customers by Offering Them an Experience – Social Celebrations: Themed and Seasonal Events."

It was also suggested snaps centering around specific adventures, touring local eateries, or performing short comedy sketches. Look around your community and among your friends for creative ideas. (wikihow.com)

Exercise: What are your first thoughts on how you can access Snapchat for your salon, skin care center, barber shop or spa?

Expert Online Resource:

www.businessacademy.com **and affiliate partner, CreativeLive, offer an expert online learning experience about growing your business** with Snapchat.

Grow Your Business with Snapchat by Inna Semenyuk

Inna Semenyuk, founder of InnavationLabs and editor of Snapchat Daily, will demystify Snapchat for small business marketers. She'll show you how to use the app's unique features and disappearing content to reach new audiences, promote your products and services in a more authentic way, and win loyal customers.

You'll learn how to target the right audiences for your business, use Snapchat's unique features and fun editing tools to advance your marketing efforts, understand the newly redesigned Snapchat, tell your brand story with disappearing photos and videos, and evaluate your Snapchat marketing efforts. BusinessAcademy may be compensated if you purchase a course.

* Copy this link into your browser: http://shrsl.com/1f8rb

TWITTER

Twitter is a social media platform where people go to connect with each other and is somewhat of a news platform. According to research, organic reach is non–existent and 53% of people never post.

Who Hangs Out on Twitter?

The President of the United States (as of 2020) is probably the most high profile twitter user. Many of his messages to the country are being found on this platform. Otherwise people of all demographics are hanging out there, but ever so briefly.

What are People Doing on Twitter?

Tweeters are restricted to a message (to send or follow another) of 140 character Tweets.

Service businesses use this platform more for customer care and social listening. People spend less than 3 minutes on the platform. An effective reach is not there yet. You can see photos, videos, and tune into interesting and not so interesting conversations.

People are looking for the latest stories, ideas, opinions, and news of whatever is interesting to them. People are basically following the conversations that appeal to them.

How Does Twitter Work?

You'll set up a profile like you do on any social media platform, so people know who you are and what you do. You'll type in your username, add your website or landing page, an engaging business bio, a good photo etc. You choose who you want to follow and interact with their information.

How Can You Promote Your Business and Make Money?

14) You can use tweets (of 140 characters) to talk about your business, manage customer service issues, promote your products and services and keep your name in front of the public. It's important to choose a good Twitter username, as it is part of your Twitter profile – the URL address to put on all of your marketing materials (where people will follow you). Keep it short, simple and memorable.

Exercise: What are your first thoughts on how you can access Twitter for your business?

YOUTUBE

YouTube is the 2nd largest search engine (owned by Google), and is the leader for video how-to and entertainment content. It's like watching TV, only it's more versatile. Comments drive interactions.

* YouTube is more of a distribution center for homemade videos.

Who Hangs Out on YouTube?

Anyone who likes to watch television or who has personal interests that they want to pursue. It's also an educational platform in the form of tutorials on many different topics.

What are People Doing on YouTube?

People are looking for information, education, tutorials, to be entertained, and for trending topics. It's pretty much *anything goes* on YouTube. Whatever your interests are, you will find videos to watch.

A lot of YouTube fans are into gaming, and some of the most widely watched channels are people who are filming themselves playing video games and/or doing comedy skits. Sometimes it's children who are playing or teens putting on makeup or motivational speakers. It's easy to get hooked on watching interesting videos and hours can be spent viewing one after the other.

How Does YouTube Work?

You can upload your personal interest or business videos for users to watch. You can also create your own channel of videos for you fans to watch. The benefit of YT is that your videos work for you every single day as opposed to FB, Instagram and Snapchat who have a much shorter time span for viewing. You'll get better exposure if you upload more than one video. Create and post a whole series in order to be seen as an expert. Got hairstyles/haircuts you want the world to see? This is the place to show off your creative talent.

How Can You Promote Your Business and Make Money on YouTube?

Please be focused on offering value to users, more than offering what you think is interesting. You are looking for your audience ... who are looking for you and your solutions. What are the questions you get from your current customers? You can videotape yourself answering those questions?

15) Along with traditional marketing, find out what content is popular by studying your competitors. What are they talking about that is unique? Can you 'one up' them? Not the expert? No problem!

Interview people you know who have an interesting perspective that your customers might appreciate.

Sunny Lenarduzzi, a YouTube expert, shares her formula. She uses the H.O.T. Script Formula: your H for HOOK gets people interested, O stands for clear OUTCOME (lets users know what they will be receiving by watching your video). Also, have a call for action, so people take the action to help themselves and you. T for TESTIMONIAL. Get testimonials from people you helped. It's credible proof that what you do helps people have a positive outcome.

16) There's a process for making videos to put onto YouTube or Instagram

- Think of a topic you are passionate about, and you are an expert in your field or industry: interesting nail designs or beard sculpting.
- Create a script or an outline of what you want to say.
- Create a teaser video and distribute that first. Make it from 15 seconds up to about 3 minutes.
- Do another longer video of 7-10 minutes. Remember, people have a short attention span and if you make your video too long, people will become bored or overwhelmed. You can do a series either on the same topic or different topics.
- Get your video set up - I film with my iphone, a tripod, ring lamp for good light, and a microphone. Don't spend a lot of money in the beginning. It can be affordable.
- Videotape yourself talking about your topic (in short segments), while also making it interesting, funny or entertaining in some way. Make sure you are in a quiet room with no distractions. Silence everything!
- You'll upload an .mp3 file from your camera to your computer where you can edit it. If you have an Imac, Imovie will work fine. Focus on the value of your content, not on production value.

People are there to see and hear you, not judge how professional your videos are. Later on you can add music and graphics.

- Upload it to YT.
- Use your other social media platforms to drive traffic to your YT video or channel. Use all your social media platforms to promote you or whatever it is you are selling ... on your website or in your offline store.
- Check in on your YT analytics to see how many clicks you are getting and when people are actually watching it.

Why Video's are Badass Important!

Facebook and Instagram have a mission to give everyone a voice and to bring the world closer together. The value in videos is that they create a shared experience and a sense of belonging.

Resources:

Use www.youloom.com for short videos. This is an app that you can download to your computer or smartphone, especially if you need practice and want to be more confident on camera.

Expert Online Resource:

www.businessacademy.com and their affiliate partner, CreativeLive, offers an online course with much more information about how to be successful with YouTube.

Build a Fan Base on YouTube by Sunny Lenarduzzi

A step-by-step guide to creating, posting, and publicizing your videos on YouTube. You'll learn how to choose the best topics based on search terms and keywords, optimize your title, description and tags for search engines and so much more. BusinessAcademy may be compensated if you purchase a course.

* Copy this link into your browser: http://shrsl.com/1f8qt

Exercise: What are your first thoughts on how you can access YouTube for your business?

17) PowerPoint slides – are a good way to get your point across with images and text, using your voiceover to speak to viewers. PowerPoint is part of the Microsoft Office Suite of tools. It's a slideshow presentation program that allows you to create, collaborate and visually present your ideas in a compelling way. I found Power-Point relatively easy and fun to use for creating visual projects.

18) PART FOUR - Create a Strategy (a focused plan) to Attract Social Media Customers

Once you know where your ideal customer is hanging out, you can narrow down the most popular social media platforms for your target market. Focus on no more than 3 platforms at a time. Once you get the attention of your target market, then start to scale (grow) your business.

- How to know where your ideal client is hanging out? Identify a problem you had in the past or a problem you can solve. Where did you go to get solutions?
- Check in to those platforms on a regular basis. You might check in everyday or so.
- Read or listen in to get an idea of what customer's want or problems that need to be solved that you can help them with. Get into their heads and pay attention to what is being said, what they use and how they think. Determine how you might help: a book, a class, a realtor, an alternative healer, or a restaurant?
- There's a website called Quora.com where you can see what questions people are asking.
- People just want to connect with others and know that they are not the only one having issues. They also want to know there are solutions to their problems. Some people don't want to be helped. They just want to vent. Let that be okay.
- Target your messages specifically to your ideal client. Remember

that it is all about them, not you. In the customer's story, he or she is the hero and you are the guide who helps them get to their destination, solve their problem, win the day or overcome stress.

- Offer little bits and pieces of information at a time (actionable ideas) to show that you are an expert. We know that you have all the answers, but don't unload on them. No one likes a *know it all*. You can be a Badass, but not too BAD!

- Let your ideal client know about you and start a helpful conversation. At the proper time, give potential customers the rundown on what you do, how you can help, and where they can find you.

- Consider posting an audio or video. Offer links to your website or YouTube videos.

- Give potential clients steps to follow to reach their goal or overcome a problem. People find it easy to follow a plan or a step-by-step system that helps them be a success at whatever is challenging them. Does you spa help customers to learn relaxations skills? Does your salon teach people how to take care of their hair at home? Does your skin care business help customers reduce or eliminate wrinkles. Help your customers reach their goals.

Examples: Here is a list of Key Marketing Assets to Build Your Business

19) These *growth hacking* examples are what you should have in place for success.
  1. **Audience-building FB ad** – see the FB section.
  2. **Flagship lead magnet** – this is a valuable piece of content you are giving away for free to get the customer's email address.
  3. **High converting webinar** – This is an in-demand webinar that is designed to attract learners and convert them into buyers.

You'll need highly valuable content that your ideal customer is looking for.

4. **Long form sales page** – When you go to another business person's webinars, you will see a long, well-written sales page that gives sales data (important info) that helps the customer see the value in purchasing their program.

    a. Typically, the longer the sales page, the more expensive the program. You're using your best marketing pitch to convince your ideal client to buy, and *to buy now* because this is a limited offer.

    b. I don't like the *scarcity pitch*, but lots of marketers use it and it often works.

5. **Free Challenge blueprint** – You can offer a free or paid *Challenge.* We talked about that in Chapter Three: The Online Phenomena.

6. **Long-term lead nurture email campaign** – This is your email campaign that nurtures your ideal client by giving them content that builds trust and a relationship over time. Free videos, audios, and tips from your blog help cement this relationship.

7. **New customer welcome email campaign** – There will always be new people joining your email list. Create a *welcome/starter campaign* (section out these new people in your email delivery program) and send them an *Introductory group of emails* that introduce you and offer specials for joining.

8. **Product upsell email campaign** – There will be content that you give away for free and content that you charge a small price for ($10-100). An *upsell* is a product that you launch to your customer base that costs more than what you usually charge. Very often it will be content that goes above and beyond what you normally offer, and it's often advanced information. The *upsell* may have some bonus material created by you or by a like-minded partner that your customer wants.

9. **Subscriber reactivation email campaign** – At some point customers will drop off your email list for a variety of reasons.

They feel they aren't receiving value, they're too busy with other things, or you're just not hitting the mark with them anymore. Once a year or so you can create a reactivation campaign to convince former customers to return. I did that in my salon.

10. **Delight your customers** - Send customers a series of emails that may attract them to new content or projects you are offering.

11. **Don't take it personal** - I've had a number of reactivation emails sent to me by a popular marketing expert that I was just tired of. I felt I had heard it all, and just wanted to hear a new voice with fresh ideas. It's not personal. That's just the way it is! * (Credit to titles by marketer, Billy Bross. Explanation by author, Linda Chappo)

Badass Important Tip #6: Test Everything!

20) One of the most important pieces of advice offered by social media pro's is *"You're Your Ads!"* Whatever you are doing online (or even in your salon, test it before you go *whole hog*. Don't put a big advertising budget into an ad or advertising budget until you know if the product or service will get some traction. Test and measure is a *Badass* thing to do!

What are the best times to post SALE content and reach your ideal clients? This is for you if you sell products online.

When is your ideal client online? What hours in the day? After work, lunch time, after dinner or late at night after the kids are in bed? If you look at your metrics you will find when the buying takes place. Often it's in the morning, during lunchtime or in the evening during downtime.

* Be consistent with your postings. Become part of their daily routine.

Working with Influencers

Many social media sites have regular people like you and I or sometimes celebrities that are called *Influencers*. They've made themselves popular through massive exposure on these sites and through their blogs. They develop a large following of fans who enjoy their personalities and opinions. You might have some customers who consider themselves as *influencers.*

Sometimes companies or corporations sponsor *influencers* to introduce and talk about their products or services, and place them in a positive light. The company gets massive exposure to people they may not reach otherwise. There is often money or perks offered in return for the *Influencer's* ability to influence the masses of a particular demographic to purchase products.

21) Here are some tips for harnessing influencers
Create a spreadsheet of *Influencers* from Instagram accounts or profiles of followers. The ideal situation is if you know that person or if they live in or near your community. Explore if this is a great person that would like and promote your products or services. Take personal information and add to your spreadsheet. Ask if the *Influencer* will feature you on their Instagram page? If they agree to post your stuff or photos, their fans will come to your page and possibly buy your products. They must tag you in photo.

Keep looking for *influencers* who you can team up with:
1. Email *influencers* your pitch. Tell them about your great product, service or brand, and how partnering with you is a benefit to them. *Influencers* generally receive perks: cosmetics, hair products, fashion, jewelry, tickets or anything free that your business can offer them.
2. Create a great subject line.
3. Asking a question often gets your email opened.
4. Start with smaller lesser-known *Influencers* (who have a smaller sized blog and following.) You have an increased chance of working with them. Again, is there anyone in your community who is popular?
5. Grow your confidence and work up to more popular Influencers.

22) How to find famous people: through their website, email address, contact page or form. Go to their YouTube channel, Instagram page, FB page and look for an email or bio. Offer special deals to your *Influencer* by making something special for them (if you have unique products).

Badass Important #7: Connect With Influencers

23) These *Influencers* are the people you want to connect with, if possible. If you know someone who actually knows an *Influencer*, talk them into introducing you. That's what a *Badass* marketer does!

When I wrote my first marketing ebook, *"How to Organize Your Marketing Campaign,"* I found out that Jay Conrad Levinson, author of *Guerilla Marketing* books (and major influencer), was in San Francisco to promote his new video. I went to the event, met him, and eventually asked him to endorse my marketing book. He did! I was happy to put his endorsement on the top of my book cover, because that's what *Badasses* do!

Badass optional!

24) Contactanycelebrity.com to get contact info of publicist or press secretary. This website says it has contacts for 59,000 celebrities. At this press time, you can pay $49 a month for a membership or $197 a year. You can get a free 7-Day Trial.

* FYI: I have not used it, and cannot vouch for their claims.

PART FIVE: Selling Your Products on Social Media Platforms

Social media platforms have opened a whole new universe for product sellers. Expand your reach through the various platforms. Before you *pay to play,* make sure your ideal customer is also using that platform.

Creating a Pre-Sale Buzz

25) Create a *Badass Buzz*, and anticipation for your sale. Announce your sale on your blog, website or offline marketing channels. Pre-market your sale by giving customers time to start thinking about what they might like.

- Direct potential customers to check your website for ideas.
- Announce *"I have a sale coming up"* on your FB page or on Instagram about two weeks before your sale.
- Use teasers, hints, or sneak previews to stimulate interest.
- Take a few photos and add impactful text, but don't tell customers everything. Feed them teasers a little at a time.
- Think about hosting a giveaway or having a contest to build buzz and get people excited. It doesn't have to be anything big, just something worth signing up for: a piece of jewelry, a small basket or bag of mystery goodies, a free haircut or manicure, a handmade craft, or a gift certificate for $$ off. It can be anything customers find desirable.
- Make a BIG DEAL out of a mystery item that will be part of your sale. Keep the special item a mystery until the final day.

Badass important Tip #8: Visuals are Necessary!
Many people are visually oriented. There are many online stock photo companies to find appropriate photos. I like a site called *Pixabay.com*

26) If you are a salon, barbershop, or spa owner, post *work in progress* photos in your blog or on your website. Give customers a reason to return, and to learn about your STORY! How did you start? What did it take to get there? What were your challenges and successes? Show your early products and how they evolved. If customers (and reporters) like you and your products or services, they are also interested in your business journey. Have you shared your story with your local newspaper yet? Get your photos ready.

27) Promote your products online and locally. Give customers a day, date, and time. Be consistent and frequent with reminders. If you are using FB, customers don't see every posting. Different people see your posts at different times of the day, so you may want to post about seven times in order to reach all your potential customers.

Systems for the Sale – Social Commerce and Comment Selling
28) "Comment" Selling: With this system, customers shop online and through social media outlets for things they want, and just comment *"sold"* or give their email address to buy directly. This system gives buyers a reason to buy your products rather than someone else's. Speak BENEFITS in your advertising copy.

Credit Card Payment System.
According to www.doughroller.net there are seven credit card processors for small businesses. Explore their website to see which one is match for your small business:
1) Shopify, 2) Square, 3) Stripe, 4) PayPal, 5) Payment Depot, 6) Dharma Merchant Services, and 7) Helcim.

29) Resources: (Ecommerce selling Systems)
1. **Spreesy.com** is like soldsie.com only it's free. They have a *Partners Program* where you can make money selling other businesses products. This is a very professional ecom-merce selling system that you can use to boost product sales.

2. **Soldsie.com** has a comprehensive blog that is worth checking out. It offers automatic invoicing. Check with the company for pricing.

3. **Shopify.com** is considered by many to be the best and most popular way to build an online store. You may use this platform along with your own brick and mortar store or use it as a stand-alone business. You can build your brand, your online presence, download free stock photos and run ad campaigns. This might be a good option for your private label products, and also to promote your salon, spa or barber shop.

Product Photography and Apps that are Creative with Photos

30) Photography is an important part of selling online if you have one or many products to sell. Like yourself, I am learning how to use a camera for photographing products and for video. In this section I will give you some tips and resources to make your products look more professional. CreativeLive.com is a great place to learn photography.

- Your photos should be consistent. Give them a consistent look and feel. Putting them on a white background (rather than color) will make them pop. Try out color backdrops. They can work in your favor as long as they don't conflict with the product colors. Test it out!

- Use your smart phone for taking photos in the beginning. Once you start making money you can invest in a better camera or a professional photographer.

- After placing your photos on your website or blog, save them on Dropbox – a cloud based platform to keep your photos safe.

- As part of your photo set up, you can buy a camera set-up for video or still shots. This is what I bought on Amazon.com. It's a tripod that has ring lighting and a place to hold your cell phone. It costs around $35 at the time of printing.

8″ Selfie Ring Light with Tripod Stand & Cell Phone Holder for Live Stream/Makeup, UBeesize Mini Led Camera Ringlight for YouTube Video/Photography Compatible with iPhone Xs Max XR Android (Upgraded)

Resources:

1. To edit your photos you can use Photoshop or software called Canva (free). Sign up with them and they send you free tutorials.

2. Another way of lighting your product is to either make your own lightbox (portable mini-studio) or buy one called Foldio from Orangemonkie ($44+) or Depthlan ($14) on Amazon.com. Prices may vary.

3. Use the Snapseed app to open the photo you just took, and go to *brush* then *exposure* and paint away gray areas.

4. There's a free app called *Wordswag* – it offers different styles of text, line spacing, and random creative ways to lay text on images. It's good for promotional events to build buzz.

Example of an Online Retail Selling Schedule

Give yourself about a two-week lead-time until your sale. It's best to work backwards from the sale date for scheduling your sales actions. This is a loose example of how to do it:

Day 1. Post a giveaway tease.

Day 2. Share what you are giving away.

Day 3 - 6. Share giveaway details – where, when and how.

Day 7. Reminder of upcoming giveaway, and post a photo.

Day 8. Post another reminder.

Day 9. Giveaway starts – give customers an opportunity to go to your website and sign up, thereby adding their names to your BADASS EMAIL LIST.

Day 10. Prime fans about your sale, "A SALE IS COMING!"

Day 11. Tell customers what you are selling and how they can buy.

Day 12. Reminder that there is a sale in two days

Day 13. Post a reminder of sale *tomorrow*.

Day 14. Announce your giveaway and sale goes live. Sale of 6 hours and then take it down.

Day 15. Afterward: thank everyone for participating and tell customers about your next sale. Schedule your next sale and start thinking about what products you want to promote.

* **Permission from *"Selling on Social: A Complete Guide"* by Mei Pak.** CreativeLive.com (See her class below!)

31) Hosting Your Online *Giveaway* (Tips, Tricks and Secrets)

- Tip: Use the word GIVEAWAY to help attract potential customers.
- Trick: Choose a giveaway product that is similar to what you are selling in your sale. This gives people who didn't win to get another chance to buy.
- Tip: Make the sale short and create a sense of urgency.
- Secret: Make it easy for customers to participate. One idea is to ask customers to *like* or *comment* on your FB post and choose a winner from one of those.
- Tip: If the photo goes viral, include a watermark or URL for people who may be tagged but who are not a customer.
- Secret: Consider turning your giveaway on FB into a paid ad. Organic reach is no longer possible because of saturation on social media sites.
- Tip: Announce the giveaway the same time as the sale.

32) Actual Sale Day: Top Tips for Badasses!

- Double check to make sure scheduled posts, photos, prices, and descriptions are accurate.
- Have *limited* quantities of what you are selling. There is *social proof* when people see others buying, like at an auction. Others want to buy because of limitations. We've all seen the *scarcity principle* at work. If there is a limited quantity, people naturally don't want to miss out.
- If you are using the Soldsie.com platform, people can see when the item is sold out. Others get put on waiting list. Soldsie.com sends an invoice to the buyer, or if they change their mind, Soldsie.com sends an invoice to the next person who is waiting.
- On *Sale Day,* be there in front of your computer to answer questions or answer on your phone.
- Explain to people who may be using soldsie.com for the first time how it works. Be there to be supportive.
- If you are using **Paypal.com** you need to send the invoice to the customer right away.
- Do a spontaneous *surprise giveaway* on *Sale Day* and choose a

random customer.

- Make sure everyone has a good experience. Have something else to offer those who didn't get in on the sale: they were latecomers, couldn't figure it out or whatever.
- **Example:** Princess Cruise Ships offer free giveaways in many of the stores and also at their Art Auctions to get people in the doors. Even though most people don't win, customers will return for the next sale and a possible surprise giveaway.

What to Do If Your Sale Flops

If your sale flops, go back and get more engagement with your fans. Take time to look at your marketing strategies, which may need to be updated. Keep testing to see what works. Fans eventually outgrow your brand, and look for other shiny objects. It's not personal! Work on expanding your reach, and get more likes on your FB page. Talk with customers to see what they are now looking for. Read the earlier chapters of this book to see if you can find solutions.

Plan for Future Sales

Get your marketing calendar and plan products, quantity, services, etc. for holidays/seasons. See my chapters on marketing for Holidays and Themes.

- If your salon or spa sells specific products, create/search new items for customers. Keep it fresh with new colors, styles, patterns, trends and different price points etc.
- Schedule your sales in advance to prevent stress and overwhelm.
- Keep customers excited about your offerings.
- Remember that you are building relationships.

USE WHAT YOU LEARNED IN CHAPTER FOUR:
TARGET SOCIAL MEDIA and SOCIAL NETWORKS

1. Be where the action Is!
2. **Part One:** You learned about Social Media and how to be a *Badass*.
3. **Part Two:** You learned about the Big 7 social media platforms: FaceBook, Instagram, LinkedIn, Pinterest, Snapchat, Twitter, and YouTube.
4. In each platform you learned who hangs out there, what they are doing, and how you can promote your business.
5. **Part Three:** You learned how to create a strategy for success.
6. **Part Four:** You learned how to sell retail products online.
7. There are 32 *growth hacks* to help you grow your business.
8. Six online learning opportunities to take your business to its next level.

Notes:

CHAPTER FIVE:

YOUR CUSTOMER IN THE SPOTLIGHT
Customer-Focused Promotions

Happy customers are the first and most important building blocks of your service business. This section is devoted to a conglomeration of *growth hacks* that can push your business forward in your community by celebrating your customer's presence. I feel that building relationships is the most fun, easy and significant part of marketing your business. You have a valuable opportunity to *reach out and touch someone* and thereby making the biggest impact! Focusing on your customers in your events and celebrations is the kindest and most generous thing you can do for them and your community.

In this chapter you'll find a large number of promotions that are primarily focused on getting and keeping customers. Don't hesitate to tweak some of the events to align with your brand.

Rock Their World Growth Hacks

1) Advertising Specialties
Advertising specialties are personalized gift items usually given to customers as promotional pieces or gift incentives. They are a relatively inexpensive keepsake, and they keep your name in front of clients. It's a good way of saying thank-you, and it creates good will.

Everyone loves something for free, especially if it's useful.

For a special promotion you could include pens, combs, calendars or rain hats with the purchase of another item. Your name and phone number embossed on the item will keep your contact information conveniently available. The most important point to remember is that advertising specialties should fit the theme of your business. For example, if you own a spa, consider having skin care samples designed with your name, address, phone and website on them.

A visually interesting logo/design may be a good opportunity to create your own personalized T-shirts, coffee mugs, canvas bags and other accessories. Sell them in your retail area, feature them in your windows and promote them in your newsletters, brochures and newspaper advertising. Give T-shirts and canvas bags to employees to use as a form of advertising.

Personalized items are also suitable prizes for customer referral contests, retail prizes for employees, door prizes and giveaways for special events.

A client of mine from Michigan was very happy to receive a really cool T-shirt from a friend and business owner in New York City. The T-shirt design was very trendy, with flashy colors and compelling images. People love to wear T-shirts with vibrant graphics. It's great publicity for your business and spreads your image/message throughout your community.

Look under *advertising specialties* for vendors in your online searches. Remember that set up fees, tax, shipping, and handling add to the total cost.

Exercise: What advertising specialties could you use to stimulate interest in your business?

2) Buddy System

Promote slow services by using the buddy system. Customers make an appointment for themselves and bring in a friend to receive the same service at half-price, or whatever discount you can offer. This stimulates business for employees or team members who will benefit from new clients.

Exercise: List your first ideas for a buddy system promotion.

Expert Online Resource:
www.businessacademy.com and affiliate partner, CreativeLive, offer expert learning experiences to help you create your marketing materials. Sign up and create marketing materials to rock your customer's world.

How to Create Marketing Materials for Small Business
by Erica Gamet

Print will never be dead, because every business needs printed marketing materials. From business cards to brochures and everything in between, this class will guide you through the creation of a suite of marketing materials to elevate your game by elevating your name.

You'll learn: design of a business card, postcard, one sheet, and flyer. You'll learn design basics for print such as file types, color and resolution, creating a cohesive look and feel for your materials that fit your style. You'll learn about getting things printed: on demand services and other options. BusinessAcademy may be compensated if you purchase a course.

* Copy this link into your browser: http://shrsl.com/1f8xe

---

3) Business Card Referral
Referral promotions begin when you give three business cards to your most influential customers, ask them to write their name on the back and give them to friends, family and co-workers. When all three cards return to you, that customer receives a free product or some other bonus. Be sure to keep accurate records. You can also send a birthday

card along with three business cards to your regular customers.

Exercise: List your first ideas for a business card referral.

4) Customer Service Representative

If you have more than one receptionist in your salon or spa, train one to be a customer service representative. He or she could take over extra duties: socialize with customers, send out mailings, make complimentary phone calls, check on promotions and advertising, or attend to anything which may better serve your business's reputation.

Exercise: List several promotional activities that you could delegate to employees.

5) Customer Appreciation Day or Week could be celebrated in many

unique ways: flowers, discounts, small token gifts to each client, a contest or a special *thank-you* mailing. I've done all of these in my salons over the years. I would draw one name of a regular customer every month and treat them to a free hairstyle and a gift. It's important to give back.

6) Customer Appreciation Certificates

It's easy to show appreciation to your most loyal customers by using these thoughtful marketing tools. It's a great way to recognize valuable customers and build customer loyalty.

Use gift certificates in three ways:

1. *Guarantee certificates* which easily attach to your products.
2. *Thank you certificates* for the most referrals.
3. *Awards* to recognize exceptional employees.

* These certificates add a degree of credibility, and show customers that you appreciate their loyalty to your business.

How to Make a Certificate

An employee who is proficient in desktop publishing can create *Appreciation Certificates* for you. You can also pick up standard certificates at an office supply store, or create specialized certificates on your home computer. Determine the image and tone you want to project on the certificate. Align the certificate with your brand image. Consistency is key!

Hints for Successful Appreciation Certificates

• Preprinted papers for your laser/inkjet printer work well. Parchment paper gives a conservative look.

• A traditional typeface such as Certificate or Gregorian are good choices. You can experiment with other typefaces to see what appeals to you, or choose what matches your other marketing materials so you have a congruent marketing system.

• Look at current certificates to get an idea of how to word them. Choose either a formal or a casual approach, again depending on the message and tone you want to project.

• The border is an important part of developing a certificate. You can use pre-printed borders or use ready-made borders from the Internet.

• Use a gold or silver foil seal to add an official look to your certificate, which can be found at office supply stores. If cost isn't a factor, encase your certificate in a simple frame.

7) Free or Paid Consultations (Building Trust!)

Consultations are a stimulating public relations promotion to offer during slow seasons. Free consultations gives customers a chance to know you before they do business with you. For some customers with *trust issues*, they want to know you, like you and trust you before they buy your product or service. Ten minutes per consultation should be sufficient.

First-time personal consultations are usually free. Attract interest by offering a *Consultation Package*, which may consist of a half hour or full hour appointment. Plan to consult with your client for 10-20 minutes, and use the remaining time for the service. It may be for a personal service such as a hairstyle, make-up, nail care, day spa massage, yoga class, or any other type of service consultation which your business offers.

Design a special consultation card for recommended products and services. Consider giving small samples of products as gifts like they sometimes do in department stores like Macy's ... *a gift with purchase.*

Always follow-up by having your receptionist confer with the customer, and make appointments or sell products.

Give a percentage off to customers who invest in your recommendations within a limited time period. Send your offer to your email list, post on social media, or on your website.

* Always mention if you have written a book, created a website or a podcast or blog.

8) Frequent Buyer Program

Follow the examples of retail stores, bookstores, and restaurants that use a frequent buyer card. Encourage repeat sales by offering customers free merchandise or services after they invest a certain amount of money. Print or photocopy 2 x 3 1/2 in. cards and include your name and squares to punch or mark with a rubber stamp.

For instance, once a customer has received 10 services, they might receive a free product or service. You could offer $5.00 off for purchasing $50 worth of product. Choose whatever incentive is appropriate for your business. Certificates worth a specific dollar amount can be mailed or handed to customers who frequently purchase a large amount of products or high-ticket services. Certificates can be easily printed on your printer.

Exercise: List your first ideas for a punch card system.

9) Gift Cards

Almost every large corporation sells gift cards to promote their businesses during the holidays, and for special events like birthdays and anniversaries. Get new and existing customers into the habit of buying gift cards for family and friends who use your services.

For example, gift cards were particularly valuable when I owned and operated the hair salon in a retirement home. Since room and board, social activities and most everything was provided (and seniors didn't need much else), family members found it helpful to give them our services in the form of a haircut, style, permanent wave or manicure gift card.

Gift cards have become a popular alternative to buying gifts that must be sent through USPS, FedEx or UPS. Customers purchase them as inexpensive and easy-to-mail gifts for friends or family members across the country. Encourage your employees to suggest gift cards at gift giving times of the year.

Order gift cards from a business supply catalog or store. You may design one with your logo, name, address, phone number and business hours printed on it. You will need them for holidays, birthdays, weddings, graduations, Mother's Day or Father's Day or anniversaries.

Exercise: List your first ideas for a gift cards

10) Introductory Service

Create interest in your new services or products by offering an introductory service for free, along with a paid service.

Customer's benefit from the free service or product, and you stand to gain a sale in the future. The business makes more money than it loses by giving away one low cost product. This may not work every time, but businesses form relationships with customers this way and increase profits.

Exercise: What introductory services could you offer to customers?

Expert Online Resource:
www.businessacademy.com and affiliate partner, CreativeLive, offer online learning experiences to help you excel in changing people's lives!

_____

How to Build and Market Products that Change People's Lives by Tara-Nicholle Nelson

Transformational consumers are the 50 percent of customers who view life as a never-ending series of behavior change projects. They're constantly looking for products and services to help them get healthier, wealthier and wiser. These people spend more than $4 trillion a year in their quest for betterment. Not only that, they're ready and willing to embark on a wild love affair with your brand.

Tara-Nicholle will share actionable strategies, marketing insights and product advice to help you better understand the human journey of the most valuable, least understood customers of our time. Highly recommended by CreativeLive. BusinessAcademy may be compensated if you purchase a course.

* Copy this link into your browser: http://shrsl.com/1f89j

_____

11) Makeover Parties
This promotion works for hair salons, day spas, facial or cosmetic businesses, and other women-oriented service businesses. Invite Women's Clubs or special interest groups into your business for makeover parties. Women love to be pampered and are generally open to trying something new. You'll charge a nominal fee for the party, depending on complexities.

Divide the party into small groups for ease of application. I suggest rotating them so one group is working with one employee, and another with a different employee. One client could be with an aesthetician, another with a manicurist, one with your massage therapist, waxing specialist, yoga trainer, and another with your computer imaging consultant. Bring them all together at the end of the session for feedback. Consider hiring a photographer to take glamorous photos of customers.

12) Advertise in local newspapers or send out invitations to club presidents. Spend time networking through your local Chamber of Commerce or various Business Women's Associations.

Exercise: List your first ideas for a makeover party.

13) Membership Club
Starting a membership club is easy and profitable (See also Membership Websites). Two benefits of the club are: a) it guarantees the return of customers who participate, and b) it establishes good word of mouth advertising.
Here are some ideas:

1. Create plastic membership cards or use regular business cards. Charge a membership fee, and offer special discounts. Be certain to establish exactly how much money your members are paying, what they are receiving, the term of the membership and any other particulars.

2. Send out newsletters or flyers to your members, describing special *members only* events and upcoming sales. Make an attractive offer to benefit your client, but also returns a profit to your business.

3. Here's another idea to implement for your biggest spenders. Remember the 80/20 rule. It states that 80% of your sales come from the top 20% of your customers. Reward that top 20% by

showing them how much you value their business. Offer these special customers an upgraded membership with special seminars, newsletters, and service or products.

4. It's important to publicize your membership club, create brochures that explain your rules, distribute flyers or posters, and, of course, encourage your employees to promote it within your business. Include info on your website and social media.

Exercise: List your first ideas for a membership card.

14) New Customers Only

Offer a special discount or a percentage off for *new customers only*. Advertise this promotion in your local newspapers, through direct mail coupons and social media. Also be conscious of having a long-time customer promotion too – so your loyal customers don't feel left out.

Exercise: List your first ideas for a *new customers only* promotion.

15) New Product Samples

Purchase *new* product samples from your suppliers and distribute them to customers. Drop several free samples in every retail bag. Make it a gift-giving opportunity, not just a simple freebie. This promotion can generate repeat sales and introduce new products. It doesn't cost that much, and everyone loves a gift or a coupon with a discount.

To inspire feedback, attach a simple questionnaire to the sample for customers to fill out and drop off. A client's opinion can contribute to your purchasing decisions.

Exercise:

1. What new products could you give away?

2. List your first ideas for a simple questionnaire.

16) New Customer Packet

To help new customers feel more welcome and valued, you may consider following in the footsteps of churches and many non-profit organizations. Create a special packet of your discounts or specials.

It doesn't have to cost anything if your budget is tight. Include brochures, business cards, special mailers, coupons, sample products or discounts on services. For your online business, email a coupon for a 10-20% off on something your customers would welcome. Everyone loves recognition and appreciation. It creates a favorable impression and says that you care.

Exercise: Make a list of items for your new customer packet or email discount.

Expert Online Resource:
www.BusinessAcademy.com and affiliate partner, CreativeLive, offer online learning experiences to help you excel in getting customers quickly. Learn new strategies today!

Turn Customers into Fans in the First 100 Days
by Joey Coleman

The first 100 days of your relationship with a customer are pivotal, and Joey will teach you how to maximize that time. You'll learn customer service best practices that consistently exceed customer expectations. You'll also learn how to track the life cycles of your customers so that you can market to them more specifically.

Joey will also outline how to apply these strategies not only to your new customers, but to your existing customer base as well. This course will give you the tools you need to transform customers into powerful advocates for your brand. Thumbs up by CreativeLive. BusinessAcademy may be compensated if you purchase a course.

* Copy this link in your browser: http://shrsl.com/1f8c

17) Passport Booklet

Create a passport booklet for your business. It looks like a regular passport, except that you stamp it when customers buy products or purchase certain services. An appropriate bonus is given when the booklet is filled. Or create a promotion based around the idea of *Passport to Adventure* or *Passport to Sales/Treasures* or *Passport to Health* or *Passport to Beauty*. Use your imagination to create something unique.

Exercise: How will you apply this idea to your products or services?

18) Phone Consultations (Coaching and Consulting)

Many lifestyle/business coaches or counselors offer consulting or coaching by phone. You can reach customers who live anywhere in the world. Connect on Skype, FaceTime, Zoom or just on your cell phone or landline. Depending on the nature of your customer's problem, you can coach or consult with customers from home, from your villa on the French Riviera or the beach in Hawaii. Set up your appointment time, payment system and any restrictions. Promote yourself on social media, networking events, your website and through *growth hacking*.

Exercise: What is your strategy for coaching and/or consultations?

19) Pre-booking

Practice pre-booking if you have a service business where customers book appointments (massage therapists, personal trainers, hair salons and barber shops). Encourage repeat visits by asking the customer to book their next appointment in advance.

For example, with a hair salon you can: a) schedule an appointment every week, b) schedule a haircut or color treatment every four weeks, c) a manicure every two weeks, and c) nail treatments and pedicures every two to four weeks. Schedule tanning sessions daily or weekly.

Set up weekly massage sessions, and shampoo and sets or blow styles every week.

This practice benefits a busy customer who often forgets to make an appointment and is without one at the last minute. Be sure to have your client's work/home phone numbers on file. When a customer pre-books their appointment, always remember to call or text/email the customer a day or two in advance to remind them. This extra reminder will cut down on no-shows. Some businesses call clients on the day of the appointment, too.

Exercise: Write a script for your receptionist to follow regarding pre-booking.

20) Pre-Pay Program

I used a pre-pay promotion in my hypnotherapy practice. This works well for fitness centers, hair salons, barber shops and spas. When a customer pre-pays for a certain number of services or treatments, you will be assured of immediate cash and repeat visits. For instance, the client receives five services over a period of time, but pays *in advance* for only four. This is a good way to build customer retention, establish customer loyalty and create interest in slower selling services.

Create a *pre-pay program card* by adding your logo, name, address, phone number and expiration date. Laminate it to keep it sturdy. Size it small enough to fit in a wallet. Optional benefits could be a quarterly newsletter and/or a discount on products.

Exercise: List your first ideas for a pre-pay program.

Resource: I found an online company that will make various custom plastic cards for your business: business cards, keytags, fundraiser cards and more. https://4colorprint.com/plastic-cards

1) Quality Customer Service

Practice quality customer service by making everyone feel welcome.

1. Be warm and friendly in person and on the telephone.
2. Always say *hello or acknowledge each client* as they walk through your door, especially if you can't get to them right away.
3. Remember to invite customers back for a return visit.
4. Follow-up phone calls to new customers are a good way to show appreciation, especially if they've spent a substantial amount of money on your product or service.

Train each employee on the importance of consultations. They must ask plenty of questions about lifestyle, likes, dislikes, career, objectives or whatever is meaningful. Several well-thought out suggestions will give the customer more options. They will appreciate the fact that you care about them.

* "Tom Marcoux, the Spoken Word Strategist and founder of GetTheBigYES.com, emphasizes, "To truly serve our clients, we need to ask questions. Merely telling a client a list of benefits is like shooting in the dark. Every benefit that is off target is only boring your client and disrupting your rapport. Sometimes, you can begin your conversation by saying, 'I'm curious. What's most important to you about …?'"

22) Brainstorm with your employees on various ways to offer better customer service. Practice with each other and give feedback.

Exercise: How can you improve your customer service?

23) Raffles

Sponsor a free raffle. Ask each customer to enter her or his name or business card in a monthly drawing or via email. Your prizes could be a service, a retail bag of products and new samples, a gift certificate, a bouquet of flowers, a new cologne sample, or a piece of costume jewelry (if you carry jewelry). I think of this as the gift that returns to you!

Ask for an address and phone number on the raffle ticket. You'll get new clients and have a new list of names and current addresses from local sources as well as from your website or FaceBook page.

Exercise: List your first ideas for a raffle, and appropriate prizes.

24) Referral Contest

Run an in-house contest for your customers to invite their friends and family. The customer who brings in the most referrals gets a prize. You can run the contest for one month or for the quarter. You'll need to keep track of their referrals and post them for everyone to see. If you have the resources, the prize can be dinner for two at a special restaurant, a week-end trip for two, a trip to a local day spa, or tickets to a movie theater, play or concert.

Exercise: List your first ideas for a referral contest.

Expert Online Resource:
www.BusinessAcademy.com and affiliate partner, CreativeLive, offer online learning experiences to help you excel in learning how to effectively run a contest!

"Contest Rules" Run Great Promotions *by Mei Pak*
Great ways to grow your audience! Promotional events are a great way to grow an audience, but if you want them to build your business it is essential you do them right.

Mei will show you how to: match your content to your goals, pick the ideal giveaway prize, collaborate with other businesses to increase entries, select the apps and tools that work best, and efficiently manage giveaways. BusinessAcademy may be compensated if you purchase a course.
* Copy this link into your browser: http://shrsl.com/1f8ov

25) Retention Marketing

Retention marketing keeps customers coming back on a regular basis. Offer new customers a discount on products or services during each visit. For instance, on their first visit offer them a 50% discount coupon (or whatever is feasible for you), the second visit they receive a 40% coupon, then 20%, then 10%, then add referral cards. If they're not your customers by this time, they probably won't be.

By all means, do not take for granted the loyal customer who has been with you for years. Show how you appreciative their patronage. Go the *extra mile* for them. From time to time, consult with your regular customers to be certain they are satisfied, and that you aren't performing services like a robot. They may be ready for a change and are uncomfortable with telling you. You may feel like an investigative reporter, but effective evaluation begins with concern and caring. Find out about their objectives so you can assist in their achievement.

If a customer prefers his or her appointment at a certain time, or on a certain day, do your best to slide them into that slot. If it's not available, reassure them that you will accommodate them as soon as possible.

Exercise: Note your first ideas for retention marketing, coupon, referral cards, etc.

26) Sampling

Follow in the footsteps of Costco, Whole Foods, and department stores. Sampling new items has been proven to increase sales. Many customers want to sample new products first before they buy. While people are shopping for items in your reception area, they may be interested in samples of hand or face cream. Sampling is an inexpensive way to create interest in your products.

Advertising on social media or to your email list is a low cost way to inform clients that you sample products one day a week or once a month. Get people into your store with a free gift.

27) Thank-you Cards

My insurance agent and optometrist both send me thank you cards, a birthday card and holiday cards every year. Sending thank-you cards to all new customers is an inexpensive, easy and effective marketing tool. It keeps you on their radar, and staying in touch may inspire customers to return more often. They'll also appreciate your thoughtfulness. Remember that as you serve your community, a by-product is increased product sales. Part of serving is also making your customers aware that you appreciate their patronage. Less expensive postcards are good too.

Exercise: List your first ideas for a thank you card.

28) Welcome Wagon

Join the Welcome Wagon to reach new community members. I joined this organization for the first year I was in business. I was a bit disappointed in the response, but that doesn't mean it doesn't work for some businesses. According to my research, Welcome Wagon no longer offers personal visits and can be found online.

Welcome Wagon is a business in the United States and Canada that contacts new homeowners after relocation, providing them with coupons and advertisements from local businesses. The company's full name is Welcome Wagon International, Inc.

Exercise: Look on the internet for your local Welcome Wagon and determine if this company is a match for your business.

USE WHAT YOU LEARNED IN CHAPTER FIVE:
YOUR CUSTOMER IN THE SPOTLIGHT
Customer-Focused Promotions

1. Put the *spotlight* where it belongs, on your customer.
2. Ways to help your customer feel wanted and appreciated.
3. Use *retention marketing* for keeping your customers as long as possible.
4. Amplify your marketing and promotions by quietly getting your happy customers to refer their friends, family and co-workers to your business.
5. You learned 28 how to *Rock Their World growth hacks* to grow your business.
6. Four opportunities for online learning experiences to take your business to the next level.

Notes:

CHAPTER SIX:

CREATE THE 'ALMIGHTY' EXPERIENCE
Attract Customers by Offering Them an Experience
Social Celebrations: Themed and Seasonal Events

There are two things people are always looking for: an *Experience* and to be *Entertained*! You'll learn how your business can participate in social celebrations in your community and walk away with new customers/friends, increased exposure in your community and a profitable outcome.

There are a few rules, and creativity that could and should be applied. Since these events are basically celebrations, they are meant to be fun, so do your best to present your events with that in mind. The better your presentation, the more fun everyone has, and you make more money. But it isn't just about the money … it's about the impact, being memorable and standing out! This chapter will assist you with some ideas to get you started.

Rock Their World Through Social Celebrations: Themed and Seasonal Events

Badass Important Tip #9
If you usually run more than one promotion at a time, post a sign in a

prominent place in your salon or on your website which says *only one discount per visit.* This should also be stated on the coupon or in the advertisement. Otherwise customers may bring more than one coupon or discount and that is a loss to your business.

Badass Important Tip #10: Include Your Employees!

Also important is letting your *staff* know you have promotions going on. Have a meeting and let them know your plans, the length of the promotion and sale prices. They are unofficial partners in your business, and it is their business to know the plan and how they will benefit.

1. I recommend that you do at least one promotion every month. You can never have too much business.
2. Remember to always use expiration dates in your promotion and advertising materials.

Badass Important Tip #11: Track Your Activities!

Don't do more activities than you can track. You want to track the results (traffic and sales) of every event so you know what worked and what didn't. It's fairly easy to see the traffic and sales happen in your store, but when it comes to your website, it's a different story. Track the analytics and conversion rates of those who click and those who buy. It is beyond the scope of this book to teach you how to do that (except through online courses and the resources section). websites sign up for their analytics from Google, who does the tracking for you.

** Review your Event Calendar in *How to Organize Your Marketing Campaign; and Hit the Ground Running"* before you begin, then fill in your dates with the most appropriate promotions to attract your target audience.

What was Old School is New Again!

To get insight on promoting your online/offline business, you can look to what I call the *Big Boys,* like Amazon, Walmart, Alibaba, Target and other corporations to follow in their footsteps. The old school promotions are still valid, and they've added a few new online ideas.

Corporations invest in, team up with or purchase companies that can build out their products or services. Currently, Walmart is teaming up with certain businesses on Shopify. Or try to find complimentary products and services to add on to your primary business.

Examples of what the social media sites promote:
- Amazon – Baby Savings Day, Prime Monday
- All stores: Thanksgiving & Christmas – Black Friday Sales, Cyber Monday
- Alibaba (China) Group – Singles Day

SOCIAL CELEBRATIONS

I'm going to start with *social celebrations and entertainment events* because they form a large part of our American culture. You can adopt most of these ideas if you promote both online and offline businesses.

When you can tie-in your business' function with social events and celebrations, you have a larger arena from which to draw potential customers, and increase your exposure. I'll cover themed promotions, seasonal, holidays, business related, ethnic, and community events – to help launch your campaign.

What is a Theme?

Have you ever heard of a *Theme Park*? Of course you have, especially if you've ever been to Disneyland, Disney World or Universal Studios in Florida or California. Each park has different themes or areas that have a specific area of focus. For instance, Disney Land or Disney World has four theme parks: Magic Kingdom, Epcot, Animal Kingdom and Hollywood Studios. Each is unique and fun in their own special way. Each one offers a different kind of entertainment experience. Disney knows how to do it right.

Universal Orlando Florida has three unique theme parks: Universal Studios, Islands of Adventure and Volcano Bay (a water park). Again, a different and wonderful experience in each theme park is the main attraction here, and draws millions of visitors yearly.

There is also Hersheypark in Hershey, Pennsylvania, SeaWorld in San Diego, California (Orlando), Kings Island in Mason, Ohio, Busch Gardens in Tampa Bay, Florida, Knott's Berry Farm in California, and many others across the country.

I've visited a number of candy stores, one in Indiana, and another in Northern California that have built out their business to be more of a *destination*. They have their products for sale as well as a factory tour for people to visit. Employees wear costumes, they have an animal mascot and décor to match. *It's a total experience!* Wineries often follow this business model.

Please remember that people want to have an *experience* and to be *entertained*. If you can meet those two requests from the public, you can inspire them to return to your hair salon, spa, barber shop, skin care center, nail salon, website or specialized property. So when you're planning your own themed promotions, plan for them to be a unique, interesting and a fun experience, no matter what it is.

1) Focus on a particular *theme* for a new event, holiday season or even for the whole year. Give each theme a tagline that identifies your business. Use it in all your marketing approaches. For example, Nike® uses one called "Just do it.™" You could also use your mission statement if it's short.
1. Be adventurous in your choice of themes.
2. Add an element of surprise to your promotions.

3.   Choose concepts that are relatively inexpensive and easy to execute.

2) AHOY MATES (All you Badasses!), LET'S BECOME PIRATES FOR THE DAY! (*Note: This event may or may not apply to the beauty business.*)

1. Consider a Pirate theme with a treasure chest full of products. Vallejo California has an annual Pirate Festival. I attended it once and it was a fun and unique experience! Lots of people were into it ... dressed in pirate costumes and acting the part. I initially thought it was a children's event, but I was wrong. This lively event was mostly adults! Someone created a giant pirate ship (with actors on board), retail booths with pirate themed items to buy (clothes, hats, jewelry etc.). One pirate even brought his parrot to entertain and talk to us. The pirate scene is engaging, probably due to the popular movie, *Pirates of the Caribbean.*

2. Use images such as swashbuckling peg legged pirates, black eye patches, gold plated loot and pirate ships in your advertising, online or offline.

3. Use images of *swords* to signify *slashed prices.* Do online research for images that represent your ideas (Google images has many from which to choose).

4. Attract new customers, and increase your mailing list by developing a contest for the pirate theme (see the online course in Chapter 5 called *Contest Rules* for more information on how to run a successful contest).

5. For example, fill a small treasure chest or jar with gold-wrapped chocolate coins and ask customers to guess how many are in it. The winner receives the treasure chest of chocolate or something similar.

6. Create a press release and give it to your local newspaper. Promote your event well, and get free publicity.

7. Promote your events to your targeted audiences on social media.

3) Academy Awards Party

This is a popular themed event that many movie watchers enjoy. You may not have the space in your salon to host an *Awards Party*. You might rent a space for the evening and invite your best customers. Or cross promote with a business owner who has the space but needs a partner to help out. You could charge or not, and offer snacks or not. It's up to you how far you want to go with this.

I know an organization in San Francisco that holds an Academy Awards party in one member's home. They make up ballots for all the different categories and charge $5.00 each to participate. The person who gets the most *wins* takes home the cash. Be a Badass, and create your own unique Academy Awards party!

Superhero Theme Days

There is nothing more Badass than *Superheroes*. People in the service industry are truly heroes. I believe we all have an innate desire to be one. C'mon, admit it! You see yourself as *saving the world!* We all think we can and on some level, we do in our own marvelous ways. Do you think Marvel™ Comics came from the word marvelous? I do, and I believe we can each be marvelous in our own Universes. And isn't that why you're here, and reading this Badass book … to become marvelous at promoting your glorious beauty business, making Badass money, and living the good life? High Five right now, you Badass business owner!!

4) Marvel™ comics and superhero movies (Batman, Thor, Wonder Woman, Spiderman, Black Panther etc.) are the BIG thing these days, and that could be an interesting theme if your business could tie in with the current movie. Here are some ideas on how to promote your business, and attract new business with a Superhero Theme.

1. Get some costumes, masks (Halloween or costume superstores or on-

line) or capes and offer to take photos of local children at a party you are hosting in your business, community or shopping center. I love to see little kids dressed up in Batman or Spiderman costumes. Well, okay... adults too!

2. Have a local cupcake or cookie shop collaborate with you, and get a discount on theme-decorated sweets to serve. Promote each other's business for the event.

3. Offer discount movie tickets to a local charity for children, and have a party beforehand. See if a local movie theater will collaborate with you during a slow time of the day/week.

4. There are many ways to promote your Superhero events:

    A. Public Relations
    B. Community flyers near schools
    C. Boy and Girl Scout™ organizations
    D. Through teachers you know
    E. Advertise in your local newspaper
    F. Write an ad for your Online Community Billboard such as Craig's List or a local online billboard.
    G. Another place to promote your event is through Next Door, a free community-based chat service.

5. Is Apple™ or another company rolling out a new cell phone or an exciting technology product? Think about a photo contest in your store or online, and piggyback on their promotional efforts. Give a prize of something you sell and promote the winner and your store. Send out press releases to local newspapers, post on social media (Instagram, Facebook) and possibly Craig's List.

Themed Promotion Exercises:

1. What themed promotions could you collaborate with?
2. What other business could collaborate with you and cross promote each other?

Tie Into a BADASS New Product Launch
Find out in advance when any new Badass product (technology, toys, dolls, bicycle, skateboard, etc.) is being released on the world stage, and tie into it with a promotion.

Resource: Television, radio, social media, your vendors, newsletters, and trade magazines are good sources for this information.

Badass Important Tip #12: Be Proactive!
Put your business in the public eye when you launch a new service or hire a new employee. Remember to be proactive, not in a coma, when it comes to getting the news out.

Expert Online Resource:
www.businessacademy.com and affiliate partner, CreativeLive, team up to bring you an expert learning experiences in *sticky* marketing.

_____

Duct Tape Marketing by John Jantsch

Join consultant and bestselling author of *Duct Tape Marketing* John Jantsch to learn how to create an easy-to-follow marketing blueprint tailored to your small business's needs. This three-day course takes the mystery and guesswork out of connecting to clients, translating leads into sales, and communicating the value of your company. Many business owners lack the resources and skills required to build a marketing plan that makes their business stand out in the crowd.

John will cover building a marketing system, creating a framework for company growth, and building your company's online presence. From spotting ideal clients to using social media strategically to gauging the effectiveness of your marketing choices, this course will give you the tools you need to feel confident implementing a marketing plan unique to your company's needs and goals. Highly recommended. BusinessAcademy may be compensated if you purchase a course.

* Copy this link into your browser: http://shrsl.com/1f8ty

SEASONAL PROMOTIONS

5) *Seasonal and Cultural Promotions* provide a wonderful way to add pizzazz, and counteract the slow times of the year where no holidays exist. When your budget allows it, do a promotion every month. Use each season or local events in your town or city as the theme for a new and unique promotion.

6) San Francisco has many seasonal and cultural events happening all the time. With a diverse population we have:

- Gay Pride Day!
- Many types of Marathons.
- Cultural Festivals in each area of the city: Italian, Chinese, Japanese and Hispanic/Latino.
- Street festivals, such as the Haight Street Fair (for those who love the 1960's & 70's), Castro Street Fair (Arts and crafts for the Gay area), and the Folsom Street Fair (for leather-related aficionados) and others.

7) Tie into local art or science museums that have special exhibits. Whether it's quilts, kimonos or the Dead Sea Scrolls, a real *Badass* can come up with something to do in their salon business to play off that exhibit.

* "The secret here is to use your imagination, and create fun and unusual promotions. Be a part of the celebration!"

8) Example: A hair salon owner in Valparaiso, Indiana used a great location and a large window viewing area to her advantage for the annual Popcorn Festival. The owner created a beach theme, and brought in sand, a beach chair, umbrella, and all the extras including a live model to promote summer haircuts and skin care products. Their promotion was a great success! I noticed it and so did everyone else.

As a *Badass Marketing Pro*, you will always tie-in a seasonal event (if possible) with other community events or festivals going on in your town or city. Create appropriate signs for each promotion and display them in your windows and throughout the business.

SPRING PROMOTIONS

9) Decorate for Spring, and make your presentations lively and colorful. Fresh flowers or large hanging plants add a bit of color and a refreshing touch to your business. Call it a *First Day of Spring* Sale.

10) Develop an interesting promotion around *the Spring Forward* concept. Use the time change as an incentive to *move forward* with a new look, nail color or barber cut. Wild and wacky clocks make fun and engaging props. Look for them on 'Google images.'

11) Use colorful balloons or banners to announce special promotions.

12) May Day flowers. It's a good time for a contest. Make up a pretty gift basket with your business products, a gift certificate and flowers.

13) Spring is a good time for a sidewalk sale for your store. Promote it on your email list and on your website. Get rid of old merchandise with an annual *Spring Cleaning Sale.*

14) A prom is another lucrative event to promote. Carry over the high school prom theme into your salon, nail or barber business. Advertise your product or services in school newspapers. Promote makeovers and tanning in your spa. Think of all the things teenagers need for a prom weekend: haircuts, updo styles, manicures or artificial nails, cosmetics etc. Promote to your email list, and on Twitter, Instagram and Facebook.

Exercise: Use your marketing calendar to PLAN every step of your promotion, and create a TIMELINE so you get it all done on time.

Online: Ask yourself or your team some important questions:
- Do you need to create an email campaign for your promotion?
- Do you need to get it out at a specific time?
- Do you need a follow up or two?

Start today to think through what you want to say, what you want to offer, and what you can incentivize for FREE.

SUMMER PROMOTIONS

15) Promote the summer season by creating a beach or resort atmosphere. Ask your employees to wear flowered shirts, dresses, sandals and sunglasses. Jamaican or Hawaiian music would be appropriate. Invite customers to join in the fun. Have a contest and offer a prize for the best costume. You may not want to do this every day, but how about on Fridays or even on the first Saturday of each month?

16) Decorate your space with brightly colored beach umbrellas, serve a fruity punch, and promote your tanning booth and tanning products. Include your email list and social media.

17) *First Day of Summer* vacation promotion. You may have a product or service that is appealing to people going on a cruise or taking a necessary vacation. Can you do a cross promotion with a local cruise agency?

18) How about a *Stay-cation?* Some people don't like to travel, can't afford to travel, or would rather just *chill* at home. This is perfect if you own a hair or nail salon, a clothing boutique add on, or a day spa. Any kind of business can provide a product or service that help customers feel good about themselves, even if they choose to stay where they are. Summer should not be just a time to work around the house, but to go out and enjoy all the wonderful things life has to offer.

19) High school and college graduation ceremonies and parties are wonderful events to promote. Use school colors, logos and pennants. Decorate with graduation hats and diplomas. Make your coupons, advertisements or direct mail look like diplomas.

20) Use the word *HOT* in all your marketing materials. Celebrate HOT August Nights (like they do in Reno, Nevada). Buy HOT new skin care products (to protect yourself from the sun), HOT new hairstyles, or HOT stone massages. You get it, eh?

21) Weddings occur all year round, but June tends to be the stereotypical hot month for brides. Your local newspaper may run a special bridal issue for wedding information. Call to find out how you can participate.

Look into local Bridal Fairs. Leave your business cards, brochures and coupons or Appreciation Certificates at local bridal shops. Bridal salons might be a good place to hawk your *beauty services.*

22) This is the time to place your ad and some pertinent information on your Pinterest Board. I'll give you resources later how to do that.

23) *Back-to-School* is traditionally the time to promote products and services that appeal to school-age children and the college crowd. Is there a campus in your neighborhood? It's a good place to slap up some posters and share your 10% off haircut sales. Post on social media sites.

24) Celebrate *End of Summer* by offering special sales. Use your point-of-purchase displays to attract quick impulse sales.

Expert Online Resources:
www.businessacademy.com **and affiliate partner, CreativeLive, offer an online learning experience to help you excel at selling at craft fairs!**

_____

Secrets of Selling at Craft Fairs: How to Get In, Make Sales, and Grow Your Business by Nicole Stevenson

Nicole has been a vendor at over 300 craft shows and produced over 40. In this class she'll help crafters make informed, strategic decisions about where to invest their time and effort. You'll learn how to: find and apply to the right show, develop your "look" using basic branding, prepare for shows with products, checklists, staff, and a pitch merchandise and display products for maximum effect and deal with pricing, permits, and taxes.

Nicole will offer insights on troubleshooting common challenges so you aren't left in the lurch without the equipment or information you need to do a great job. You'll also learn strategies for keeping in touch with customers and building relationships with event producers that last long after the show ends. Big Thumbs UP! BusinessAcademy may be compensated if you purchase a course.

* Copy this link in your browser: http://shrsl.com/1f8oh

_____

FALL PROMOTIONS

25) Use autumn colors in your business for a Fall season theme. Promote the *First Day of Autumn* by decorating with autumn leaves, pumpkins and cornstalks.

26) For cosmetic industries, this is a good time to promote seasonal cosmetic colors, such as the darker and sienna colored lip and nail colors.

27) Use your wacky clocks again for a *Fall Back* promotion based on the *turning back of the clock*.

28) It's a good time to do a *Fall Preview* of new products or anything unique you've picked up at a Trade Conference or ordered from vendors.

29) Remember to do a big promotion for *Halloween*. It's always a good time to have fun, dress up in costumes, and remember the *spirits of the season*. Post your party or costume contest on your FB business page.

WINTER PROMOTIONS

30) The Winter season is a great time to promote *Christmas* gifts, product and services, and winter accessories (In Chapter Seven we will go into more detail about the holidays). Customers either head for the slopes or warm weather resorts, so offer *vacation packages* at this time. Create a themed promotion that is suitable for whatever weather is prevalent in your area of the country.

31) Take advantage of the Holiday season to promote specialty items or to discount anything that hasn't been selling. Do a search on Amazon to see what the popular items are, and get a few of those into your retail mix.

32) Decorate with snowflakes, ski photos, snowmen, or polar bears. Spray snow onto your windows to give the illusion of a fresh snowfall. It's nice to see if your location doesn't have snow.

33) Offer a special price on a service or product, or have a contest.

Exercise:

1. What seasonal promotions would be profitable and fun for your business?

2. What seasonal promotions would be attractive and fun for your customers?

Seasonal and Themed Exercise:

1. You are a *Badass Genius!* Select one of the seasonal themes and use your own creative genius to make it unique to your business or industry.

2. What themed promotions would be profitable and fun for your business?

3. What themed promotions would be attractive to your customers?

Notes:

USE WHAT YOU LEARNED IN CHAPTER SIX:
CREATE THE 'ALMIGHTY' EXPERIENCE

Attract Customers by Offering Them an Experience
Social Celebrations: Themed and Seasonal Events

1. Customers are looking for experiences and entertainment.
2. The Yearly Marketing Calendar keeps your business focused on your goals.
3. Social celebrations, both themed and seasonal make people happy.
4. You learned 33 *growth hacks* to grow your business.
5. Two opportunities for online learning experiences to skyrocket your business's traffic and profits.

Notes:

CHAPTER SEVEN:

PROMOTE THE HIGHLY PROMOTABLE
Monthly Promotions & Holidays

Customers prepare themselves mentally and financially to spend money during the holiday seasons. Don't let holidays go by without acknowledging them. Use these tips to make your holiday season more prosperous for you, your business and your employees.

1) Create an exciting atmosphere for *buying* by decorating your small business in festive colors.

2) Use interesting props. Look for a rental company in your town or city that rents unusual props.

3) Plan in advance to purchase additional decorations for Holiday promotions, if needed. Be smart and pre-buy needed items when they are on sale.

4) Pre-package retail products for quick and easy sales. Put slow selling items together.

5) Tie in a contest or special price promotion.

Exercise: What interesting seasonal promotions can you offer online?

6) Ask your employees to join the party by dressing in a fun way.

7) Show your commitment to holiday celebrations by having some kind of celebration in your salon. Promote *a discounted item* to your list too.

I attended a Christmas gift show one year where I had access to lots of retail items. I bought items at enough of a discount that I could re-sell them for a fair price. I purchased handbags, scarves, jewelry and more at a great discounted price. Look online for gift shows that may be happening in your area. The one I attended was in October, just in time to order for the Holidays.

Expert Online Resource:
Business Academy and its Affiliate partner, CreativeLive, offer online learning experiences to help you excel! This online course is for Badass Growth Hackers!

_____

Smart PR for Artists and Entrepreneurs by Ryan Holiday
Get the right kind of attention. Getting free media attention is a powerful and often misunderstood communication tool. Join media strategist and best selling author Ryan Holiday for his course on how to create smart, savvy and provocative PR campaigns.

Ryan's course will teach you how to get the right kind of attention, without paying for it. Take your business to the next level with proven strategies and techniques. Highly recommended by CreativeLive.
* BusinessAcademy may be compensated if you purchase a course.

* Copy this link in your browser: http://shrsl.com/1f8th

_____

JANUARY PROMOTIONS
8) Do a New Year's promotion using a celebratory theme: party hats, streamers and horns to announce a new service or product. Choose an item or items that could use a boost or you want to eliminate from your stock. Offer a discount if your product looks worn.

FEBRUARY PROMOTIONS

9) St. Valentine's Day is an easy holiday to celebrate. Red hearts and cherubs set the theme. I offered chocolates to my customers, and gave out single roses to the ladies.

10) This is a good time to promote *Gift Certificates*. Get one for Mom, Aunt Ellen, your sweetheart, your sisters, your teacher, or those special friends who are supportive all year long.

11) Promote *Sweetheart Services*. Buy one and get the other at half price, or charge full price and offer a rose and/or candy. For boutiques, this is also a good time to sell jewelry, perfume and cosmetic or nail services.

12) If you promote a contest, you could giveaway a **Dinner for Two**.

13) President's Day is another reason to show your patriotism. Bring out your flag, decorate in red, white and blue, and offer a special sale on products. Get your email list involved with your sale.

14) Consider offering a 10% discount on all product packaging with the colors red, white and blue. Or think about putting red, white or blue stickers or flags on items you want to sell.

15) February is also **Black History Month** and it's a good time to celebrate prominent African Americans in your community or tie into national events. Tune into television stations that offer documentaries, and features on the African American Experience.

MARCH PROMOTIONS

16) Most major cities like Chicago and New Orleans celebrate **St.**

Patrick's Day like there's no tomorrow. You can be part of this *Badass Buzz*. Celebrate St. Patrick's Day, and decorate with leprechauns and green shamrocks.

17) Play Irish music in your business, and offer sale prices on all products with green colored packaging.

18) March is **Woman's History Month,** a good time to celebrate outstanding women in your life, your business and your community. Tune into television stations that offer documentaries and features on the *Woman's Experience*. Share those with your customers.

19) March Madness is a popular event for college basketball fans. Many fans tune into the NCAA Division of this tournament, which has been played annually since 1939. Promote this event in your barber shop.

APRIL PROMOTIONS

20) Easter is another fun holiday to promote. Decorate with Easter bunnies, baskets and candy. My customers loved it when I gave away a nice Easter basket or two. I bought three very festive Easter baskets from a popular candy store, and drew the names of three lucky winners. (As a side note, I built up my mailing list with this contest.) Or take a more serious approach and decorate with Easter Lilies.

21) Celebrate **April Fool's Day** with a *Foolish Promotion,* using your imagination on this one. You can do it right ... you're a Badass Marketer, right?

Example: April Fool's Day is a yearly holiday that can also be a themed event. *Example:* There is a town in Occidental California that has an *Occidental Fools Parade!* They have a parade (with a marching band) where families in this picturesque town in the redwoods dress up as *fools* and parade their silly way down the main street in town, ending up at the Occidental Center for the Arts. Viewers can experience frivolity, bands, music, crowning of the *King and Queen of Fools*, and more. You will see *Zero the Clown* standing on the *Podium of Impossibility* and other such foolishness and great fun.

Exercise:

1. What can your spa or salon business do to entertain your customers and townspeople to cash in on a themed or holiday event that brings new people to your business?

2. What can you sell?

3. What value can you offer?

4. How can you create an entertaining experience?

5. How can you impact your community with a special event?

MAY PROMOTIONS

22) Mother's Day is one of the biggest holidays of the year.

1. One year I celebrated Mother's Day by giving a carnation to every mother who entered my business. Another year it was a rose. They appreciated the acknowledgement.
2. Appeal to mothers by offering a discount on attractive services or products.
3. Advertise gift certificates for customers to give as a gift to their mother or to a woman who is *like a Mother* to them.
4. Display photos of your employees' mothers.
5. Have a contest for entrants to write a poem for their mothers in 50 words or less. Give a prize or gift certificate to both the winner and his/her Mother!

23) Memorial Day is another patriotic holiday in which to celebrate the veterans who served our country, living or not. This is a good time to bring out the flags and the red, white and blue decorations. It's a time to show where your heart is.

JUNE PROMOTONS

24) Father's Day is a good time to promote men's products and create interest in gift certificates. Run your promotion the full week before Father's Day. If possible, you could also display and highlight photographs of your employees' fathers.

25) Father's Day Contest: Have a contest for entrants to write a poem for their fathers in 25 words or less (or more!). Give a prize or gift certificate to both the winner and his/her father! Think about videotaping the poetry reading, and sharing it on YouTube or your website.

26) Weddings or Engagements: June is always a time to acknowledge engagements, weddings, brides, grooms, and everything else involved in the event. Hair and nail salons, skin care centers and barber shops call all get in on this event. Promote your services at your local high schools or on social media. Most couples make their plans a year or more in advance, but keep putting yourself out there for those couples who decide to wed at the last moment. They will be forever grateful.

27) Graduations: June is the typical month for graduation parties, so if you have a product or service that would appeal to the new graduate or their party, then this promotion is for you and your business. You can offer:

- New Hairstyle for the girls
- Haircuts for the guys
- Skincare for the girls: make up, eyebrow arching, facials

- Manicures or artificial nails for girls

Exercise: What service or product can you offer for graduation parties?

JULY PROMOTIONS

28) For your **Independence Day** promotion, bring out the flags, picnic props and patriotic colors. Many people are out of town or busy for the holiday, so begin your promotion several days before the Fourth of July celebration.

29) Many people enjoy a *Christmas in July* celebration. Be a Badass entrepreneur and host or hostess this *pretend* celebration for your customers. If your part of the country suffers with summer heat, this option might be a welcome escape.

AUGUST PROMOTIONS

30) There aren't any holidays in August, so this is a good time to offer your **Back-to-School or End of Summer** promotions. If you have a boutique or a retail area, you can present your new items, or offer discounted prices on shampoo and conditioners, skincare, and suntan lotions.

Hair salons can offer Back to School haircuts, perms or neon hair coloring for a Badass new look.

Expert Online Resource:
www.businessacademy.com and affiliate partner, CreativeLive, offer expert online learning experiences to form powerful habits.

The Power of Habits by Art Markman

Setting a goal is one thing, but actually doing the work to achieve that goal is a totally different endeavor. If you want to hit your targets and make lasting changes in your life, join author and psychologist Art Markman, Ph.D. This course won't serve up superficial self-help tips. Instead, you'll dive into the latest cognitive science behind behavior change.

You'll learn how to build new, positive habits and break the cycle of existing negative ones. You'll explore what it takes to sustain healthy habits over time and increase your chances of maintaining new habits. Big Thumbs up! BusinessAcademy may be compensated if you purchase a course.

* Copy this link into your browser: http://shrsl.com/2050p

SEPTEMBER PROMOTIONS

31) Celebrate **Labor Day** with a *sidewalk sale* to attract people who are off work and strolling through your neighborhood.

32) A **sidewalk art show** could be fun, or hire a student to dress up as a clown and giveaway balloons in front of your business. Send a promotional email to your list and add it to your social media campaign.

OCTOBER PROMOTIONS

33) Columbus Day is a National Holiday celebrating the anniversary of Christopher Columbus's arrival in the America's on October 12, 1492. Use your fall colors or appropriate decorations to participate in a Columbus Day sale and celebration.

34) Coupon Book: Get local merchants to participate in a coupon book.

Coupon books are a good way to get local businesses involved in cross promoting. You may also attract customers who may not be aware of your business.

35) Halloween was always a joyful time in my salon business. I loved to decorate with ghosts, goblins, witches, pumpkins, fake cobwebs and black and orange crepe paper. My employees always dressed for the occasion, and handed out candy. We loved the look on our customer's faces when they entered the business. Halloween wasn't necessarily a moneymaker for my business, but a *feel good* celebration of the season. Celebrate this beloved holiday in any way that appeals to you.

NOVEMBER PROMOTIONS

36) Thanksgiving is always the start of a very busy holiday season. Decorate with fall colors, turkeys, pilgrims, cornstalks and more. Hot apple cider is a nice treat for walk in customers.

37) Black Friday is one of the biggest shopping days of the year. Right after Thanksgiving is a good time to bring out your newest or most popular products and sell, sell, sell! Start soon enough with social media and your own promotions and you can compete with Amazon, Walmart, Target and other big retail sellers who don't carry your unique merchandise mix. An *in-store experience* will most certainly attract customers if you plan it right.

38) Use the Election Day theme to run a *Politically Correct* promotion. Decorate with signs, buttons and banners from all parties so you don't appear partial and alienate people who support another party. Use caution when doing this so customers and staff don't find themselves in a conflict. You can put up a heart shaped sign, *"Love One Another no Matter Who You Vote For."* * You could stay neutral and not mention it.

39) Veteran's Day is another opportunity to offer a sale, themed promotion or just an acknowledgement to local veterans. Flags and red, white and blue banners honor the Veterans still living and those who remain in our memories. Be creative in getting veterans into your store.

DECEMBER PROMOTIONS

40) The **Christmas** season was always the most prosperous time for my service and retail business in general. Sales get the biggest boost of the year. Get customers in the buying mood by decorating in a big way with a tree, some decorative displays, red ribbons, and snow-covered windows. Prepare pre-wrapped gifts for those who need another last minute gift. Add some holiday cheerfulness to your website by changing some font colors or adding holiday photos.

41) Ask your employees to wear red clothes or Santa caps to amplify the season. You can provide fun props that bring a smile to your customer's faces.

42) Start early and stock plenty of your favorite retail gift items. Add colorful baskets filled with small stocking stuffers. Place impulse items on the desk or in a visible place.

43) Always heavily promote your fragrances and jewelry at this time and stock plenty of gift certificates.

Exercise:

1. What holidays are especially appropriate for your business?

2. Make a list of promotions you can do related to monthly events.

Badass Important Tip #13: Submit Your Ideas - Get Valuable Exposure!

Do you *Badass Growth Hackers* have any interesting information you'd like to contribute to this section? Submit it to businessacademy10@ aol.com and give us permission to use your submission in our next printing of this book, along with your name and business name for credit and exposure. Thank you in advance!

USE WHAT YOU LEARNED IN CHAPTER SEVEN:

PROMOTE THE HIGHLY PROMOTABLE
Monthly Promotions and Holidays

1. The value of monthly and holiday promotions for your business.

2. The value of monthly and holiday promotions for your customers and community.

3. You learned at least *43 Growth Hacks* for your business.

4. Two online learning experiences to excel in growing your business.

Notes:

Notes:

CHAPTER EIGHT:

YOUR BUSINESS IN THE SPOTLIGHT
Your Business-Related Events and Celebrations

One of the most powerful ways to learn about hacks for growing your business is to create your own newsworthy event and/or participate in local community events. Business celebrations are an excellent opportunity to show your barber shop, spa, nail or hair salon off. Whether your business is new, or has been in existence for a while, you can create unique opportunities to attract new or past customers. In this chapter you will find 10+ growth hacks.

IT'S PARTY TIME FOR THE BADASS ENTREPRENEUR
1) Any business's marketing endeavor needs to include four events that celebrate the business's existence, and place in the community:

1. Your Grand Opening or Annual Open House
2. Your Business's Anniversary
3. Your Educational Events
4. Your Part in Community Events

When you're ready to part-tay, decide on a date, a plan and an execution strategy. Decide on a date at least two months in advance so you can line up your list of attendees, invitations, snacks (catering), music, publicity, decorations, promotional items, and employees.

1. Write the copy for your invitations, email list and social media campaign.
2. Do your best to get free publicity for these most important celebrations. Send out a press release to local media and follow-up right before your event.

PART ONE: CELEBRATE YOUR BUSINESS'S GRAND OPENING OR ANNUAL OPEN HOUSE

Once all the preliminaries are designed and prepared; send invitations, decorate to the hilt, offer refreshments, plan a contest, and do your best to be the *Badass Growth Hacker* that I am training you to be.

2) If you have enough space in your business for your **Open House or Grand Opening,** consider sending out party invitations to local businesses (preferably the media), and to high profile customers. There are many ways you can go about this, depending on your budget and ambition. If you don't have the space, put on a smaller gathering for your most valued customers. You can do it up nice with sparkling wine, sparkling water and cheese and crackers if your finances are tight.

3) This is one of the most important events or celebrations your business undertakes. To make your grand opening *the talk of the town*, create a memorable event! Purchase extra decorations and flowers. You might even find a flower business that will consider trading flower arrangements (cross-promoting) in return for products or services. If you don't ask, the answer is always *no!*

4) Make your salon look impressive for first-time visitors. Appetizers and refreshments are generally part of the grand opening festivities. You may even offer door prizes, and give away a few services or products. Consider hiring a DJ or live entertainment (if affordable).

5) Hack Your Entertainment: Do you have a nephew or friend who plays a pretty decent guitar, or a granddaughter who plays the piano and has a portable keyboard? Do you know a good local singer who would like to perform in order to get free exposure? How about your local high school jazz band? These are all *Badass Hacking* possibilities. Sounds cheap? So what! Give people a chance who need the exposure. They'll be forever grateful, and they might pick up a gig through your event, plus a nice generous tip from you or others.

6) Have your entire staff dressed up and available to welcome guests, make them feel comfortable, and answer questions. **The business they drum up from selling future appointments/products can actually pay for the event.** (Train your staff on what to say and do. Provide them with a script.) Hey, anything is possible for a *Badass Growth Hacker*!

7) Send out a **press release** or write an article for your local newspaper. Include a photograph of your staff in front of your business, or doing styling, manicure or a massage within your business. If you have the resources, hire a professional photographer. The *Lifestyle* section in your local newspaper or *Craig's List* is always a good spot to display a grand opening event.

Write who you are, and make *your story* compelling. Talk about your location, any interesting history or facts about you, your business or your employees. Include a list of services, products and operating hours. This is an opportunity to get coverage or exposure, so make it GOOD!

8) How about a **gift drawing or even gift bags?** You can purchase little chochkeys with your name on them to give away. Your name will be a nice reminder of the event and your business. Over the years I bought rain caps, pens, combs, hand lotion, magnets, and various other items to give away (with my salon's name or logo on them).

Attend any trade show and you will find large companies giving away little incentive items that are a gift but also a reminder for future business. Include your name, phone number, website address, email address or whatever will fit on the item.

* Have plenty of impulse products in high profile areas and gift certificates on hand.

Exercise:
1. Note your first ideas for a newspaper article advertising your Grand Opening.

2. Plan a Grand Opening or Open House for your business (decide on invitations, target market, media, costs, refreshments, entertainment, and social media).

Expert Online Resource:
BusinessAcademy.com and its affiliate partner, CreativeLive, offer expert learning experiences to help you excel! Learn to be bold and beautiful while meeting new people!

The Art of Meeting and Greeting People
by Daniel Post Senning

Always know what to say and do when meeting someone for the first time. This course tackles the ins and outs of introductions, first impressions, and initial conversations, so you can walk into potentially difficult situations feeling confident, knowing how to act and never at a loss for words.

You'll learn how to: Introduce yourself and others gracefully, extend and build on introductions, know what to say and what not to say in conversations, listen to people so they know they're being heard, shake hands properly in the era of hugs and fist bumps, handle a situation where you don't know or forget someone's name, and discuss personal topics that require the most care and tact. Business Academy may be compensated if you purchase a course.

* Copy this link into your browser: http://shrsl.com/1f8zg

PART TWO: CELEBRATING YOUR SALON'S ANNIVERSARY

Since statistics say that most businesses fail within three years. You have the *Badass Growth Hacker* right to gloat over surviving the statistic. I did! Every year on my anniversary I celebrated like a Rock Star! Follow the same guidance for your anniversary as you do for your initial open house.

When I was impulsively fired from my frustrating pre-salon job (for starting my own salon business), my former employer sarcastically remarked, *"You won't last two years!"* After my two-year business anniversary I raised my glass to him (with champagne), *"that I was thankfully not working for him anymore!"* I was a success on my own. I sold that business after fourteen years (and traveled the world), and altogether owned three highly successful hair salons.

I consider myself a *Badass serial entrepreneur,* so I also owned a catering company, a hypnotherapy practice, and BusinessAcademy. com (my online business school for entrepreneurs). Not only that, I'm not done yet. I plan on (someday soon) starting a non-profit organization. It's on my bucket list. It's a very *Badass* thing to have goals and achieve them!

PART THREE: YOUR SALON'S ANNUAL EDUCATIONAL EVENTS

9) Put together an annual or bi-annual educational event or seminar that is specific to your business. Promote it to your local offline or online community. Is it an educational seminar, a retreat, a webinar,

an interview of someone of influence, or an introductory open house for your business? What are customers asking for: a new product, service or additional content? What problem needs to be solved? A *Badass* innovation-oriented business owner will be the first to show them the ropes. No fear!

Educational Events to Drive Traffic to Your Salon:

1. Plan a theme.
2. Invite your best customers.
3. Design a memorable event.
4. Get your staff on board to greet customers, help them feel at home, and answer questions.
5. Get a video recording of your event and promote it on YouTube, Instagram, your website or anywhere you want or need exposure.
6. You may be able to sell your video on educational platforms like Teachable, Udemy or Coursera, or on your membership site. I say, *"Go for it!"*

* Depending on the type of business you own, and your ambition, you can have a good time with this idea, and win new customers in the interim. Use social media and your email list to promote this event.

Exercise: What unique business-related events could you sponsor?

PART FOUR: YOUR SALON'S PARTICIPATION IN COMMUNITY EVENTS

10) Almost every community sponsors **Local Celebrations and Special Events** to provide entertainment and community for their local residents. These events also offer local business owners an opportunity to serve food and beverages, sell arts and crafts, provide musical and various entertainment, promote non-profit ventures, and give exposure to many other retail operations.

- Events that were popular where I grew up in Northwest Indiana were the Popcorn Festival, the Blueberry Festival, the Wizard of Oz Festival, the Diana of the Dunes Festival, and the Grand Prix Jamboree, an auto race created by my friend Jim McKamey.

- Whiting, Indiana even has a *Pierogi Festival*, and I've been told it's one of the biggest and most popular festivals in the area. Who would have thought? But there's a large population of ethnic Polish people in the area, and lo and behold, they love their Pierogi! Those events are always well attended, and even draw large crowds. If you are in the area, it is recommended to go, eat, enjoy! Yay, Pierogi!

- Where I live now in the San Francisco area, **people celebrate music** with jazz, blues and reggae festivals. Then there are cultural ethnic festivals, the Ethnic Dance Festival (which I love), local wine, arts & crafts festivals, Harvest Fairs, Shakespearean Fairs, The Cherry Blossom Festival in Japantown, the Chinatown parade and festival, and neighborhood street fairs.

- There are yearly celebratory fairs in the Haight Ashbury district of San Francisco (home of the *Summer of Love*), and the Castro Street neighborhood, where the LGBT (Lesbian, Gay, Bi-Sexual and Transgender) communities get together to celebrate their *Pride Week* with a parade and street fairs.

- Each neighborhood has it's own annual street fair, as well as marathon races. Before Christmas there is a *SantaCon* event, where many people dress up in unusual Santa Claus outfits, and celebrate the season in a way only San Franciscans can do.

- Another favorite of mine is *Literary or Book Fairs*. San Francisco and Berkeley, California have yearly literary festivals where famous writers and authors come to teach and share their knowledge. You can have your book signed and questions answered. It's great fun!

135

- All of these events and more are opportunities to reach masses of potential customers if you sign up for a booth or even share a booth with someone, if that is allowed.

Exercise: What community events would be profitable and fun for your hair, nail or skin care business?

Expert Online Resource:
ww.BusinessAcademy.com and our affiliate partner, CreativeLive, have teamed up to bring you an expert online learning experience, with industry experts and reasonable prices.

_____

Simple PR: Pitch Yourself (Your Product) by Brigitte Lyons

Building a presence as a thought leader and influencer is a powerful way to attract clients. An appearance in publications and programs your target demographic likes and trusts is an ideal way to build your audience.

Veteran PR expert Brigitte Lyons will help you develop a framework for establishing expert authority and getting covered by the press. You'll get insights on developing your voice and *expert* bio and how to tie those efforts back to your business. Brigitte will detail the range of opportunities available – podcasts, webinars, media interviews, etc. – and help you tailor a pitch for each of them. Get Brigitte's Bundle! BusinessAcademy may be compensated if you purchase a course.

* Copy this link into your browser: http://shrsl.com/1f8xk

_____

IMPORTANT: Do you Badass Growth Hackers have any interesting information you'd like to contribute to this section? Submit it to **businessacademy10@aol.com** and give us permission to use your submission in our next printing of this book, along with your name and business name, which we'll include if you like. Thank you in advance!

11) One of my favorite Growth Hacks is *"Word of Mouth!"*

There's no better growth hack than the forever FREE *word of mouth,* offered by satisfied customers. When you do everything right, or nearly right, people will talk about you and your business in a positive way. You can find proof of that on Yelp and other community sounding boards like Foursquare, TripAdvisor etc. Another popular way to get referrals is through your local online *Next Door!* Otherwise your local networking buddies, friends and family are a good source for getting the word out about your product or service.

Train your staff to talk about your salon in a positive way. It doesn't matter if they are salespeople or not. They should know what you excel at. People know people and everyone you pay should be a supporter of your product or service. Your business and their jobs depend on every-one spreading the good news about what product or services you offer that may change people's lives for the better.

12) Loss Leaders are highly used Growth Hacks

Lots of big merchandizers and Big Box Stores use *Loss Leaders* to get traffic into their stores. They know that taking a small loss on one or two high-in-demand products will attract buyers who will most likely pay full price for other products. Let's face it, we've all gone to a store for a particular sale expecting to save money, yet we walk out with many other items not on our list.

This strategy pays off in big ways by attracting customers to your salon or website for that product, as opposed to them going to another salon to buy that item. Not only that, next time the consumer wants something similar, they are apt to look at your promos, website or marketing materials first. First is good, right?

USE WHAT YOU LEARNED IN CHAPTER EIGHT:
PROMOTE THE HIGHLY PROMOTABLE
Monthly Promotions and Holidays

1. How a *Grand Opening* and / or *Open House Celebration* helps you get seen in your community.
2. How celebrating your business's anniversary is a statement of success.
3. How offering educational events keeps your customers engaged.
4. How participating in community events builds status.
5. You learned 12 *growth hacks* to grow your business.
6. Two expert online learning opportunities to promote your business.

Notes:

CHAPTER NINE:

DRIVING TRAFFIC ON A DAILY BASIS
Business-Focused Promotions

Entrepreneurs who are serious about growing their business, through growth hacking, do something every-day or at least once a week to drive traffic and sales. They're business-focused! Whether it's creating a powerful message on your answering machine, writing blogs, or attending business net-working events, consistent marketing can build you an empire.

Attending industry conferences and educational events are a must, and they're fun too. I always attended conferences (Chicago, L.A. and San jose) for upgrading my skills and knowledge.

Another great option for growth is to talk to your local vendors. Having a good working relationship with your salespeople can some-times offer valuable insight. They see what's going on in salons in your town or city, in your state, as well as in your industry. You may or may not like what you hear, but vendors can be an eye-opening resource.

This chapter has 39 easy and affordable *growth hacks* that you can pull from to promote your entrepreneurial venture.

1) Your Business Answering Machine
Your answering machine can be a powerful marketing device, but keep your message short so you don't irritate customers who may hang up

out of frustration. We've all experienced *voice mail HELL* while trying to get to the right person. Don't do that to your customers.

2) Consider turning on your answering machine for after hours' calls. Use it as an advertising message center in which to state your days and hours of operation, and your location. Your answering machines' message could act as a running advertisement for new services or product specials.

If you want to receive only short messages, you can set your machine for a one minute message setting and inform the caller *"you have about one minute to leave us a message. Thank you."*

* I wouldn't suggest letting customers leave a message to cancel by phone, if that is a consideration. You want to have the opportunity to reschedule and not lose the business.

Exercise: What message would be appropriate for your answering machine?

3) Awards Ceremony
An annual *Awards Ceremony* is a great way to present recognition certificates to your employees or outstanding customers. Make your business's awards ceremony a fun and memorable event with invitations, decorations, publicity, refreshments and music.

Since *growth hacking* is the name of the game, you can save money by handing out invitations rather than mailing them, decorating with inexpensive crepe paper, and serving homemade cookies or cakes. You can use your stereo for music or a local music student.

Exercise: What awards could you give away, and to whom? (Employees, suppliers and clients?)

4) Your Own Calendar Promotion

The advantage of creating a *knock-em-down visually-oriented desktop or wall calendar* is that your customers will look at it every business day for twelve months. That's a full year's worth of promotion for your business.

Be creative as you produce a calendar that appeals to your target market. For an eye-catching visual piece, have a professional photographer take photographs of twelve of your best and most creative images that highlight your salon or spa. Ask employees or customers to be models or participate in some way.

As a less expensive alternative, use humorous clip art, famous quotations, or interesting photographs. Use a selection of beautiful, unusual papers for an aesthetic quality. They can be printed at your local big box store.

You might fill-in some of the dates with a friendly reminder about product or service promotions. Offer specials or monthly coupons. (Refer to your yearly marketing calendar) Leave plenty of space if you want your customers to write on the calendar. Remember to personalize it with your logo, address, phone number and hours of operation.

Always plan ahead for your calendar. Discuss with your graphic designer how long it will take for design and printing. You will probably want your materials ready by the following year for Christmas. If you feel uncomfortable about planning so far ahead, you might want to add a note on the cover, requesting customers to confirm events over the telephone.

As an alternative to the high cost of mailing calendars, you could send out postcards or emails inviting customers to pick up the calendar in person. This practice gets random customers into your business.

• Visit a card shop or bookstore to get more ideas for creative calendars.

Exercise: To develop a calendar, please respond to these questions:

1. List your first ideas for a calendar.

2. Choose a goal. Is it designed to impress your customers, to inform them of your services, or to remind them of your business?

3. Do you want it to hang on the wall or sit on the desk?

4. Do you plan to mail it or hand it out?

* Look online at printing companies to find the best prices for your calendar.

5) Hacking Contests

Contests are a fun and effective way to create interest in your business. Have two kinds of contests: one for your customers, and another for your staff.

- Chapter Five offers an online learning experience in contests, called *Contest Rules.* Check it out, and learn the rules!

- A customer-centered contest allows your customers to participate in the growth of your business. Advertise the contest in your printed materials, and remember to add the deadline, date of drawing and the amount of prizes. The mailing list created by your contest can be used again for your direct mail promotions.

- List the winners' names on a flyer in your salon, photograph them and publicize the event in the newspaper.

- Implement your in-house contests for employees only. Give gifts or recognition awards to employees who surpass sales quotas or dramatically improve their performance. I gave a monetary prize to the employee who sold the most retail products that year.

6) Five Great Reasons to Promote a Contest:

1. Develop a current mailing list.

2. Attract new customers into your business.

3. Build goodwill.

4. Give back to the community.

5. Create new publicity for your business.

The Prize: Give away a service or a package of products. If your budget allows it, give away new products, spa services, or lunch at a local cafe. A gift card for a cup of gourmet coffee is appreciated or two movie theater tickets for a special night out. Offer a small token to everyone who comes in to enter the contest (an incentive gift like a pen), or just confine it to several larger prizes. It's your choice!

• Prizes should be commensurate with the amount of effort required.

Exercise:

1. What are your first ideas for a contest?

2. What are your first ideas for prizes?

3. What media would you use to promote it?

7) Co-op Advertising

Co-op advertising is essentially a partnership advertising arrangement. Product manufacturers (or vendors) who want you to be successful with their new products may offer co-op advertising. Their advertising department will provide you with professional looking ad slicks and radio announcements. You'll place the vendors' advertisement along with your salon's name, address and phone number in your local newspaper or on the radio station of your choice. Radio advertising is still popular, and your area may or may not have a local newspaper.

The benefit of using vendor technology is that the manufacturer will return to you a portion of the costs you incurred in the form of customer credit. You'll apply the credit to the purchase of additional products. Sometimes reimbursement is in the form of a check, but not usually. Co-op advertising may or may not be available in your industry. Speak to your vendor or salespeople about the efficacy of this type of promotion.

Exercise: Which product manufacturers offer co-op advertising?

8) Coupons or Groupon

Use coupons or an online source called Groupon. I will cover both options in this section. These are two different and effective sources of advertising. It has been determined that, according to marketing statistics, your response rate will increase when using a couponed ad rather than a non-couponed ad.

Create Your Own Coupons

How to Word Your Coupons:

Send a *response* message to the reader by including the three favorite selling words: *"money, save and free!"* Each coupon should have a clearly defined offer, such as *Two for the Price of One* or *Get $5.00 off on a $50.00 Purchase*. You can use the offer as your headline.

For more creative ideas, notice the ads/coupons that you receive in the mail or through circulars. Place coupons at the bottom of the page and use dashed borders around the box to draw attention. Always give your coupons an expiration date. Include any limits.

Put coupons in newspapers, booklets, online, in your email lists or distribute them individually. You can put them in the shopping bag along with retail purchases. Check first before putting your coupons on windshields in the parking lot. Some towns have an ordinance against littering.

Exercise: Sketch your first ideas for a coupon.

Digital Coupons

Groupon is a middleman service that promotes restaurants and stores. In return, they earn a commission each time a customer purchases a coupon. Apps notify potential customers of deals your salon offers. There are *Deals of the Day* and *Getaway Deals* that attract customers.

Subscribers may forward a deal to their friends that could possibly go viral on social media. Some deals are relevant for a couple of days and others are valid for six to twelve months.

You can advertise through Groupon or become an Affiliate Partner and earn money that way. See the websites lifewire.com or www.groupon.com for information on becoming a seller.

* I haven't used this platform, so I recommend asking other salons in your industry about their experience. Also, see if there are any nearby businesses who sell through this vendor. Your neighborhood may or may not attract Groupon buyers.

9) Cross-merchandising and Cross-promoting

Cross-merchandising is a great way to introduce your new salon, spa or nail salon to existing businesses in your town or city. Find businesses that compliment yours. Through this collaborative event, both businesses win.

Print Appreciation Certificates or coupons offering a special discount, and send them to local businesses such as fitness centers, boutiques, yoga studios or any others. Call them first, as they might like to trade certificates. Invite them to offer your coupons as gifts to select customers.

Cross-promote with nearby businesses (maybe in the same shopping center?) and hold joint sales. The advantage lies in sharing the cost of print advertising. Reap rewards from a wider variety of participating businesses. Cross-promote around a holiday or special event.

10) Offer a Prize. You'll attract more customers by holding a drawing during this promotion and giving away a grand prize. The shopping center where my hair salon was located gave away a television. It was a nice incentive to get residents to offer their contact information and return to the center.

Online marketers call those people *leads*. They may or may not buy the first time, but with the exposure you offer, there is a good chance they will return. This is also a great way to increase your mailing list. Remember to use social media to promote your business.

Exercise: Which local businesses can you align with for cross-merchandising?

11) Door Hangers
Printed door hangers are an inexpensive way to advertise your newest products and services.
1. Avoid having too much information on the hanger because customers are turned off by cluttered and wordy ads.
2. Use large bold lettering with plenty of white space.
3. Use any extra space to add a *money off* coupon, or a free gift (sample packet of products, small gift items, newsletters and more).
4. Offer a *mystery gift* to each customer who returns to your business with their door hanger.

* Customers come into your salon to shop, and the door hangers are returned for you to use again.

Exercise: Write out your first ideas for a unique door hanger.

12) Flyers and Postcards
Flyers and postcards are effective, inexpensive ways to promote your services and products. Postcards have the added benefit of lower postage rates, easy labeling and lower printing costs. Provide an

appealing offer that is limited by an expiration date. Always ask for the sale!

Give flyers and postcards a large visual or headline, and information on your promotion. If you are located in a shopping center, the merchant's association will often promote its businesses with a flyer. You won't have as much space to advertise, but you'll receive more exposure.

The flyer or postcard should state the name of your business, the product and service offered, your business location, hours of operation and telephone number. Add coupons onto flyers too.

Brainstorm with your staff for new ideas to implement. Create your own unique designs on your desktop, then send your artwork to a printer. I like PS Print.

13) There are several ways to **distribute flyers and postcards;**
1. Hand them out to customers (in their bag) and people on the street.
2. Mail them to your target market (direct mail).
3. Staple them to community bulletin boards.
4. You can distribute them at trade shows (I've done it).
5. In the case of my former target market, hair salons and stylists, I keep targeted postcards in my purse and drop them through the door's mail slot if the business is closed.

As an alternative to a strictly serious promotion, create visual impact and interest by:
1. Drawing funny or interesting illustrations (caricatures).
2. Enlarge the names of products you offer.
3. Use a map (on one side of flyer) to identify your business location.
4. List your newest employee or service.
5. Include your favorite recipe.
6. Add your statement of philosophy or mission statement to focus on customer needs.

Exercise: Write your first ideas for a postcard or flyer promotion.

14) Graphic Design Books and Magazines

Graphic Design books are the epitome of innovative and forward thinking advertising and promotions. If you or someone from your staff has desktop publishing experience or graphic design skills, you can find unique promotion and advertising ideas at bookstores, magazine stores or thrift stores that carry graphic design magazines.

Graphic design professionals regard these books as a compilation of the year's best advertising designs. Choose several ads that impress you and appeal to your target market. Recreate them (with your personal touches) on your computer or take them to your graphic designer as potential ideas. You may even find some pretty good design books in a used bookstore.

* Advertising experts suggest that you continue to use an advertisement that people are responding to. Don't change an ad because it has become boring to you.

15) Grocery Stores

Your regional grocery stores may offer discount couponing to local businesses. Business people buy advertising space on the backside of shopping receipts. Offer a coupon or discount, and keep track of results to determine if your promotion was successful. Call businesses to learn their success rate.

Exercise: What local grocery stores offer receipt coupons?

16) Hotels/Motels and Tourist Agencies

Local hotels and motels are good places to leave business cards, brochures or information. You'll get a better response if they allow you to leave your information in the rooms. There may be a charge for this service. Set up a cross-promotional deal with local tourist agencies.

Exercise: What local motels and hotels could you target for your campaign?

17) Info-graphics (Handy Tip Card)

An info-graphic image tells a story of sorts. It helps you to make a point with valuable information quickly and visually. These are great for blogs or Pinterest. They should visually convey information that your ideal client wants to know. You can purchase info-graphics and other graphic design images from a company called www.designcuts. com for use in your promotions and branding.

18) People like to read handy tips. List 5-10 tips to do something in a better, easier, smarter or more cost effective way. Photocopy your list on a card along with your business's logo, name, address and phone number. Hand them out as a gift to customers, or include them in your brochures or advertisements. Use a catchy image.

19) If you have a **Pinterest** account for your business or want to start one, you will find that learning info-graphics is a good creative way to drive traffic to your salon or website. Look on Pinterest for ideas or you can also look on the internet under *info-graphics* for lots of great ideas. Look on the www.designcuts.com website to purchase pre-made images for you to edit to your specifications.

Exercise: Use your expertise and develop a handy tip card (list three ideas for this promotion).

20) Re-activate Inactive Customers

Look through your files and periodically target inactive customers with postcards or your email blast. Offer a discount or free gift to encourage a return visit. This idea can also be implemented during slow times of the year. I notice that I often get added back onto an email list that I previously asked to be removed from. It's okay to give them another try.

Re-activating inactive customers can be an inexpensive way to add to your email list or in house clientele. If they liked your products or services in the past, they may change their minds and like you again. Give it a chance.

Exercise: List at least five inactive customers who would benefit from this promotion.

21) Low Tide Promotion
Run a low tide promotion. Offer your discount coupons during slow periods of the year to encourage in-salon visits, phone calls or website visits. This is a good time to run specials, repackage products, or promote something new and interesting. Advertise in newspapers, send out flyers or use a local radio station.

Exercise: List your first ideas for a low tide promotion.

22) Midnight Madness
The shopping center where my salon was located promoted a Midnight Madness Sale once a year. This was always a big event for us. All stores were open from 9 pm to midnight. We offered a hair-cutting discount, and it was a huge success. But as years passed, discounting became the norm, so that promotion was no longer as successful. Perhaps you can use one of these *growth hacks* to grab the attention of your community?

Exercise:
1. What other merchants would you contact to promote a Midnight Madness Sale?

2. What product or service could you discount for this special sale?

Exercise: List local motels/hotels that would be an appropriate target

150

for your advertisements.

23) Online Bulletin Boards

Use Craig's List or other local online bulletin boards to promote your salon or spa. Post your products or services in the areas of Community, Services and For Sale. What's appropriate for your biz?

24) Point-of-Purchase Displays

Point-of-purchase displays help stimulate the sale of new products and provide strong brand identification. These are great for boutiques, hair salons, spas and barber shops.

Put your manufacturer-created displays in a place of high visibility since they contain the newest products. Set a small display on the desk, a front showcase or anywhere within view of clients.

Showcase retail products in the front window, but be aware that the sun will eventually fade your displays. As long as it's still stylish and not shopworn, you can rotate the display with others to give a fresh perspective. Use the aesthetic advantage of coordinating your professional displays with your salon atmosphere. Keep a consistent image.

* Dramatic displays contribute a feeling of prestige to your business. Many displays include samples or trial products. Encourage your clients to sample new products.

Exercise: List your first ideas for point-of-purchase displays.

25) Video Product Knowledge

Buy a used computer for your waiting area and videotape a commercial for your newest products or styles. You can think of them as *in house tutorials.* They benefit your business in three ways: they heighten interest, detail products and boost sales performance. Showcase your services or products in a positive light, educating your customer in a predetermined manner. These effective marketing tools are designed to make sales easier for you and your staff. You can post the same video on YouTube, your blog or FaceBook etc.

Exercise: List suppliers to call for this information.

26) Product Labels

Attach a label with your salon's name and phone number to every product and item sold. It doesn't need to be a private label product. Preprinted product labels constantly remind the customer of your business, and your phone number is always at their fingertips. Product labels can be found in mail order catalogues.

Exercise: Note your first ideas for a product label.

27) Promotions Binder

Promotional binders are a good place to keep copies of your advertising and promotions. A simple reference file will keep ideas from past promotions at your fingertips. You can return to it periodically and redesign some advertisements that didn't convert, or re-implement some successful promotions which you may have forgotten.

* Another purpose for a binder is to keep track of interesting and informative clippings from newspapers and magazines. Use them in your newsletter or share them on social media platforms. As a reference, include a selection of other businesses' advertisements for fresh innovative ideas.

28) Posters, Banners, Tee Shirts, Hats and Bags

A poster advertising your salon or spa (grand opening, anniversary, holidays, etc.) can be costly, but it's a nice way to present your image visually to the public. Unique posters can be sold for a nominal fee, or used as a prize in a contest. They can also be distributed to local businesses for public viewing.

A unique image can also be put on T-shirts, baseball caps or canvas bags. Sell them in your salon, on your website or on social media sites. Use these images in your Pinterest info-graphics.

The elements of a terrific poster or retail items are:

1. A simple layout with large type or bright colors that can be viewed from a distance.

2. Include your name, address, phone number and website.

3. Use one dominant element: an image or headline.

4. Choose colors that evoke an emotion or create the right mood.

5. Determine size and shape by deciding the poster's display location.

Exercise: Write your first ideas for a unique poster or retail item.

Private Label Products

29) Stand Out From the Crowd with Private Label Products

The specific purpose of private label products is to give you an opportunity to have your own line of cosmetics, shampoo etc., by attaching your business's label on the front of manufactured products.

Private label companies are generic companies who create products and sell them to small businesses. They usually create or formulate cosmetics or bath products. Sometimes they are located in the U.S., but most often in China or another foreign country. Their goal is to help you create a following by offering your own (line of products) brand, as if it were created by you.

The quality of the product varies and you should do the research, ask for testimonials, sample the products and compare prices before you make a purchase order. You may also create your own formula for your private label products.

30) Use a **certificate of authenticity** for your private label products. Guaranteeing the effectiveness of your products is particularly useful for new or private label products. These are products (shampoo, conditioners, lotions, skin cream, nail polish, hair spray or anything) that are consumables; products that customers purchase over and over.

Choose your partner company carefully because they become your brand with your name on the product, and you are accountable for its effectiveness and safety.

Badass Important Tip #14: Choose Appropriate Products!

A *Badass* salon or spa owner will make certain their customers are really interested in purchasing the products. You don't want to be left with a ton of unsold inventory. Give away some samples in the beginning to customers who you feel would give you honest feedback. In that way you'll have a testimonial and a customer for the product.

31) Restaurants as a Source of Promotions

Investigate local restaurants, typical family establishments, who offer *placemat advertising*. Disposable paper placemats are designed with various size ads from local businesses. You'll be charged by the size of your advertisement. There may also be a charge for designing the ad. Call the advertiser for more details. There may be alternative ways to cross-promote with a local café or restaurant, depending on what kind of business you own. This is call B2B or business-to-business advertising.

* Make sure the company you are dealing with is reputable. Call them and ask questions. Don't pay upfront!

Exercise: Which local restaurants could you target for placemat advertising?

32) SALE Items

Almost everyone is attracted to a big SALE sign. Remember to properly plan for the sale, and don't underestimate the sale's potential. Don't embarrass your business by not having enough *sale items* on hand when you need them.

I once worked as a seasonal employee at a large department store that ran out of important cosmetics right at Christmastime. Many sales were lost and it was frustrating for employees to make a sale then look in the drawer to find no products.

Follow in the footsteps of grocery stores by putting your sale items in a shopping basket. People love to rummage. These ideas worked for me, but don't use this hack every week — once every 4-6 months is enough.

Exercise: List items that could be put on sale immediately.

33) Telemarketing

There are several advantages to using the telephone as a marketing tool: to increase customer service and promote new products or services in a more personal way.

Show appreciation by calling new customers a few days after they purchase a service or high-ticket product. It's a good time to get feedback. Also, any complaints can be handled discreetly over the telephone. You can create loyal customers when you handle their complaints with care.

Exercise: Write your first ideas for a script to increase customer service.

34) Testimonials or Reviews

Testimonials are your most valuable assets when it comes to building and growing your business. Almost everybody reads them before they buy any product or service online and offline. Websites like Yelp™ is based on reviews. Customers are more discriminating than ever and a great testimonial can sway a purchase in your favor over your competitors.

Collect testimonials from satisfied customers and use them in your social media campaign, on your website, in brochures, advertisements, press releases, direct mail and any other promotional materials. There's nothing better than a satisfied customer to persuade other people to become satisfied customers.

Exercise: What three customers would write a testimonial for your hair or nail salon, spa or barber shop?

35) Theaters

A. Live Theater Brochures. Reach your local consumers through live theater productions. Theater customers generally scan the program while waiting for a performance to begin. Local theater groups often have reasonably priced advertising space on the back of their programs. Call their office for a quote.

Exercise: Which local theaters could you target for an advertisement?

B. Movie Theater Advertising. When we go to the movie theater today, we not only see the favorite blockbuster, but we are also forced to watch commercials. A lot of the big corporations blast their auto ads, soft drinks, food snacks and other things on the big screen.

Small neighborhood theaters can be a novel source for marketing your salon, spa or massage business. Many movie theaters use promotional slides to entertain viewers while waiting for the show to begin. You can advertise and reach a large audience with this media.

36) The best way to measure your response rate is to require the ticket stub in order to receive a discount. Check with the theater manager for possibilities and a cost quote.

37) A local theater in San Francisco cross-promotes with a nearby ice cream store. A movie stub will get you a free ice cream cone when one full priced cone is purchased. Explore creative ideas.

Exercise: Which local movie theaters could you target for an advertisement?

38) Warehouse Sale

Everyone loves a SALE! Have a Warehouse Sale and people will associate your salon with others who are successful with this promotion.

Create your own Warehouse Sale inside your salon or spa. Follow in the footsteps of big box, grocery and drug stores. Purchase cases of products, cut the box tops off, and stack em up!. It's a great way to promote certain products. I used this promotion once a year or so with great success; hair spray, shampoo, brushes etc.

Exercise: List products that would be appropriate for a warehouse sale.

Box-Building Your Successful Business

Now that you've been exposed to many new (and some old) ideas, begin by incorporating some of them into your own marketing campaign. Remember, you don't need to include everything. That would be overdoing it!

I used most of the promotions in this book, but it was over a time period of about fourteen years. Just choose the promotions that you believe would work for your business and give you a good **ROI!** (Return on investment)

Exercise: Please respond to these questions regarding your promotional activities:

1. What results do you expect from each promotional effort?

2. How will you assess the amount of response you receive per

promotional effort? How can you make it better?

3. What three actions will you take to create value for your salon, spa

or Internet business?

4. What three actions will you take to create value for your customers?

5. What three actions will you take to create value for your employees?

6. List your first ideas for driving your retail business UP.
Target Date:

Master Your Mindset

Don't just read this information, but take steps to put some of these ideas into practice. Conquer procrastination, perfectionism and self-doubt. These three distracters will hold you back from taking steps forward and from succeeding at what you are meant to do. Don't let fear get in the way. Take baby steps forward. Being prepared helps you to become more confident, and confidence breeds' empowerment and success. You've been given all the tools to succeed. Please use them.

Expert Online Resource:
www.businessacademy.com **and affiliate partner, CreativeLive, offer you an expert learning experience to break the habit of self-doubt.**

———————

How to Break the Habit of Self Doubt by Mel Robbins

1. Use Mel Robbins' five-second rule to stop negative thoughts and change your life for the better.
2. De-escalate anxiety and agitation.
3. Create mental scripts that help you overcome typical situations that get you into trouble and prevent you from acting.
4. Overcome your mental blocks and change the way you think about things.

* Copy this link into your browser: http://shrsl.com/20521

———————————

BusinessAcademy may be compensated if you purchase a course.

USE WHAT YOU LEARNED IN CHAPTER NINE:
DRIVING TRAFFIC ON A DAILY BASIS,
Business-Focused Promotions

1. How to use focused ways to promote your salon.
2. Methods for a direct reflection on your business.
3. You learned 38 *Growth Hacking* methods to grow your salon, spa or barber shop.
4. One expert online learning opportunity to promote your business.

Notes:

Notes:

CHAPTER TEN:

YOUR COMMUNITY IN THE SPOTLIGHT
Community-Focused Promotions

These *growth hacks* and community-based promotions are the ones that may draw local consumers into your salon and your event. It's important to do a certain amount of outreach in your community and these ideas (some free or low cost) are a good starting point. To build momentum, I recommend continuing with your community-based events each year. People will come to expect your event and look forward to it. Through word of mouth, others will find out for *free*!

1) Plan a Block Party
One community-focused event is a *Block Party*, where the merchants in a town or shopping center get together and promote their businesses. Block parties are more effective when a number of merchants equally share the cost of print advertising and whatever work needs to be done. The merchants can share their mailing lists, which give all merchants a larger pool of potential customers.

2) Get together and make it an annual event. All the merchants can donate door or raffle prizes. Attract a large crowd with a sidewalk sale, a carnival, special craft booths, art show, food, clowns or special entertainment. Develop a theme and a name for your block party.

* Expectations breed excitement. Your annual block party will continue to grow in size and reputation. Condition your community members to expect this extravaganza every year, and most importantly, require everyone to participate. Give each merchant an assignment, otherwise they may blow off the event, and you'll do all the work.

Exercise: What local merchants would be interested in promoting a block party?

3) Charities and Fund Raising Events

Supporting charities and participating in fund raising events are an easy and inexpensive way to gain visibility and promote your business. You will not only have the opportunity to establish valuable friendships and gain exposure, but to network and gain personal gratification.

Find a charity you feel strong about and create an event to support it. Talk it over with your staff, volunteers and customers who may be interested in participating. You will be raising money and feeling joyful for giving back to a worthy cause.

Exercise:
At what local charity can you volunteer your services?

4) Churches

Many churches offer their congregation a paid membership that includes discounts at various local businesses. Take advantage of this opportunity to get extra exposure, new clients, more sales, and who knows, maybe even a few extra blessings from *Beyond the Clouds!*

Exercise: What churches could you call to offer a special discount?

5) Fashion Shows

Fashion shows are a fun opportunity to connect with community members, often through churches, fundraisers and business development.

Develop a rapport with local clothing stores or department stores. Offer to participate in their seasonal fashion shows. Churches, boutiques, department stores and community organizations sometimes put on fashion shows as charity fundraisers. Tie in your product or service to this event.

Promise to use your social media following to promote the event so they choose your business and not your competitor. If it's *your* boutique's fashion show, videotape your show and present it on YouTube, other social platforms or on your website.

Fashion show promoters often place promotional information at table settings. Put together gift bags to give to women's clubs' fashion shows. It's a great incentive to drive traffic to your salon or spa. You can fill your own personalized *goodie* bags with product samples, discount coupons, promotional items,business cards and your business brochures. It's a great time to network with the community.

You can also set up a panel discussion on hair, nail and skin care trends, along with a fashion show. Videotape that too. People love to know what's going on in the fashion world and how they can wear the latest fashions. Use it on social media ... YouTube.

Exercise: What women's organizations or businesses can you align with to participate in fashion shows?

6) Festivals and Local Festivities

Local festivities are a good way to connect with people in your community, especially those who have never heard of your salon. I talked about this a little bit in a prior section, but I'd like to include more information here, especially for new salon owners who may have some fear of reaching out. Local festivities offer an opportunity to increase business traffic.

***

Investigate your local or nearby Chamber of Commerce or newspaper listings about local arts and crafts festivals, circuses, carnivals, county fairs, marathons or auto races. Identify when they take place in your vicinity.

Many towns and cities create large festivals around a particular product, which is indigenous to the region such as: wine, blueberries, popcorn, garlic, pumpkin, or others. How can your salon tie into these events or products?

Some festivities revolve around music: jazz, blues, bluegrass, symphonies, or others. If the Olympics or similar athletic events take place near you, take advantage of the extra traffic flow. Introduce your services to visitors coming into your town for the day or weekend. Target local campgrounds and hotel or motels for extra advertising.

Create a compelling visual for your promotions which fits into the theme of the event. Use it on all your advertising, particularly on flyers or posters which feature the event. Crate an email campaign for your event and follow up on social media.

Exercise: What local festivities can you participate and promote your business?

7) Networking Groups

Use networking groups to connect with people in order to share contacts, information and missions. Your local Chamber of Commerce, Mall Association, Professional Business Women's Associations and local business associations are good starting points for networking. The people you meet can refer you to other effective organizations.

These events are popular for business owners to meet other business owners, and get the word out about what they are doing. It's a social event, often with food/snacks and beverages as a way of drumming up business and supporting other business owners who may be just starting out.

Bring plenty of business cards or brochures and be ready to

socialize, network and possibly team up with another business. There is sometimes an entry fee.

I recently went to a local Women's Networking Event where there were snacks, beverages, an opportunity to greet and meet as well as a goodie bag from the promoters. There may be a place to display your cards and brochures. About 30 of us stood in a circle and briefly gave our names and pitched our businesses. A couple of entrepreneurs set up tables to sell jewelry and cosmetics. One member offered *palm readings,* which was an unusual but interesting addition. Everyone loved the idea and lined up to have their palms read.

***

The individuals who join these groups enrich each other's lives and businesses by supporting each other and sharing resources. Speak authentically about your business and its benefits. You'll receive the most value by keeping in contact with the people you meet. Keep a record of your contacts, the date you met them, what they do, and the name of the organization. Enter your new names right away into your email contact list. Keep it handy for those important referrals.

* Tom Marcoux, the Spoken Word Strategist and founder of GetTheBigYES.com, says, "When you begin a conversation while networking, ask people, 'I'm curious. How do you help people?' Demonstrate your caring first. Wait for a question like, *"What do you do?"* before you launch into a description of your business."

In networking, you're helping other people to fulfill their needs, too. When you become aware that a client, friend or employee needs a particular service, refer them to someone you've met through a networking group. Ask them to mention your name when they contact that individual.

Effective networking can be fun and rewarding on a personal level as well as a professional level. Send thank you notes to networking contacts who refer new customers to you.

Networking is something I do on a regular basis, more as support than for actual business sales. Sometimes I make a connection and will get business, but I find that business owners are there mostly to sell and not to buy. I could be wrong, but that has been my experience. So, I still go to events with an open mind and just try to enjoy myself, make connections and be truly helpful.

Women's workshops, trainings and networking events are great places to connect with business leaders. I'm a happy camper if I walk away with a few helpful tips to grow my business or content to pass along to you. With that said, I have made lifelong friendships with people I've met at networking events. We are like-minded and are a good support system for each other.

Exercise: Which networking groups or business associations can you join and support?

Expert Online Resource:
www.BusinessAcademy.com and affiliate partner, CreativeLive, offer you an expert learning experience to help you build your network.

Build Your Network and Dream Career by J. Kelly Hoey

A strong network is one of our most important career and business assets. And yet, most of us relegate networking to the bottom of our to-do list. If you want to pursue your dream career, networking must become a priority. But how do you know where to begin? How do you build strong relationships in an authentic way? And how do you get over your deep-seated fear of putting yourself out there?

You'll learn how to build your network and reach out to people with confidence. Discover what you want and where you're going, map out your linear or nonlinear journey, navigate career crossroads and passionately pursue uncharted path. Find high-quality connections in every aspect of your life. Highly recommended! BusinessAcademy may be compensated if you purchase a course.

* Copy this link into your browser: http://shrsl.com/1f8zn

8) Newspaper Articles, Trade Journals or LinkedIn

Writing informative newspaper articles for your local newspaper is an attention getter, especially if you are an expert in your field. As a powerful tool, the written word gives you the opportunity to educate the public. Make a point of stating any benefits of using your business.

Submit articles to trade journals or specific content to online companies (LinkedIn) who are part of your industry. Many magazines have special category editors who do most of the writing for the magazine, but you might be able to break in with a lively or unusual article of consumer interest.

9) Public Personal Appearances can be Cash Cows

If you enjoy public speaking you may consider making personal appearances at women's clubs, men's clubs, church functions, sorority parties, senior citizens' groups and charitable affairs. This can be a lucrative field for people who are experts, and speak with humor and enthusiasm.

High schools often invite local business people to speak on *Career Days*. You will most likely do this for free when you are just starting out, but many public speakers make very good money speaking on certain topics and/or teaching at local or corporate events. Take your valuable knowledge and recycle it to other areas, and make more money.

The more well-liked you are, the more money you will make, especially from referrals. There is also the possibility of selling other helpful items in the back of the room during breaks or after the event.

It is always wise to maintain a visible profile in your community. Don't wait for someone to ask you to speak. Contact groups who have an interest in hearing speakers.

If you are not comfortable with public speaking, perhaps an employee would enjoy the opportunity? The entire business staff could join forces and take turns speaking about who they are and what benefits they have to offer.

Always be on the cutting edge of what's happening in your field or what is trending in the moment and how you can tie that in with your expertise. You'll have fresh ideas to share with public speaking groups and your customers.

If your business offers personal services such as cosmetics, image consulting, fashion coordination and other applicable services, consider offering a *before and after* show for these organizations.

In a former salon, we presented a *hair fashion show* at a luxury lakeside restaurant owned by a client. My employer emceed the event. He sang songs and entertained the audience while we styled our models. We performed quick makeovers using pre-planned models and audience volunteers. We impressed the audience with our efficient and effective quick-change techniques, and in return, received a wonderful free dinner and cocktails.

Exercise: Make a list of names and phone numbers of places where you could make a public appearance.

10) Senior Citizen's Day

Attract the attention of your communities' large senior citizen population by offering discounts or services they find helpful ... wellness or health care. Grocery stores, movie theaters, hair salons, golf clubs, senior centers or wellness communities, etc. offer a savings or activities to seniors.

Exercise: List the names and phone numbers of nearby senior citizen centers.

1.

2.

3.

4.

5.

11) A Monthly or Bi-monthly Sidewalk Sale

Sidewalk sales are an inexpensive promotional tool. You need do very little advertising other than word-of-mouth and flyers. The tables out in front of your business provide a good way to mark down and get rid of all your overstocked and shopworn merchandise.

Add your brochures, price lists and business cards to the table. Use signs to encourage shoppers to come inside your business for additional sale items.

Exercise: What items would be appropriate for a sidewalk sale?

12) Athletic Sponsorships

A good way to get community recognition for your business is to sponsor local sporting events: little league, a softball league, a bowling team, or other event. Beauty contests are another area that may get your business publicity and your name in the newspaper.

* On the other side of the coin, you can look for sponsors for your business event.

Exercise: What local groups could you sponsor? Or who could sponsor your business?

Notes:

USE WHAT YOU LEARNED IN CHAPTER TEN:

YOUR COMMUNITY IN THE SPOTLIGHT
Community-Focused Promotions
1. How participating in Community Events is good for business and for you.
2. How community participation can attract your ideal client and more.
3. Use what you learned from the 12 Community Participation *Growth Hacks* to grow your business.
4. One expert online learning opportunity to promote your salon, spa or barber shop.

Notes:

CHAPTER ELEVEN:

HONORING THE RELIGIOUS AND ETHNIC HOLIDAYS
Promotions to Celebrate Cultural Diversity

Your salon business can participate in many ethnic and religious holidays. Because these holidays and events are highly personal, choose those that are of interest to you or that you have a passion for. Your salon may reside in an ethnic neighborhood where you may want to honor and celebrate your customer's heritage.

You could participate in whatever way you feel comfortable or you might reach out to someone in the community for guidance.

1) Religious and Ethnic Holidays

You will find some of the holidays listed here, and since this is not a book about religious and ethnic holidays, I am merely observing them in this chapter because they are important to many people and they may also be important to your business and community. If you have a serious interest in learning more, I suggest you do some online research to get more clarity. I have not included dates, because they sometimes change from year to year. Rather than make an error, I recommend that you check online to see the exact dates of any religious or ethnic holidays.

2) The United States and other countries: Americans and many other countries celebrate religious holidays, often the offshoot of *Pagan* holidays. Business people and many Americans think of our religious holidays as *commercial* holidays, or an opportunity to make money. It's okay to sell and provide the gifts that people want for themselves and their loved ones.

We must remember that these are actually religious holidays for many people and not opportunities to spend money they don't have. For Christians, *Christmas and Easter* are their most important religious holidays, and if you can tie into that feeling, then you have expanded your reach on a heart level.

3) Jewish Holidays are *Rosh Hashana, Purim, Pesach, Shavuot, Tish'a B'Av, Yom Kippur, Sukkot, Shmini Atzeret, Simchat Torah and Chanukah.* There are also minor holidays as well. I'm not familiar with all of the Jewish Holidays, but if you are interested in celebrating these holidays and others in your salon or spa, you may want to do some research on the customs, restrictions and dates. I've had the wonderful opportunity to participate in a couple of the Jewish celebrations/rituals and found them to be quite touching and compelling.

4) The Hispanic and Latino culture celebrate *The Day of the Dead,* when people in that culture honor their ancestors. There is often a parade of people dressed as skeletons/masks and they may have a meal in the cemetery near their departed loved ones.

5) According to my research, there is also a year of celebrations in Spanish-Speaking countries; *Día de los Reyes Magos, Día de la Constitución (Mexico), Las Fallas de Valencia (Spain), La Semana*

Santa, Cinco de Mayo (Mexico), Fiestas Patronales de San Salvador (El Salvador), La Tomatina (Spain), and Día de Muertos. There is also the *Carnival (celebration) and las posadas.* Honoring loved ones who have passed away is a powerful statement on the love of family.

While living in San Francisco near the Mission District, which is primarily Hispanic, I enjoyed the experience of *Day of the Dead*, and found it to be an equally fascinating experience.

6) The Chinese Population in the U. S. has their own festival celebrations. Here are some of the most celebrated festivals in China: *New Years Day, Laba, Spring Festival, Chinese New Year; based on the Chinese Lunar Calendar, Lantern Festival, Qingming Festival, May Day, Dragon Boat Festival, and Double Seventh.* Chinese celebrations are always colorful, dynamic and a joy to watch. * The Spring Festival is celebrated by other Asian countries.

7) Brazil celebrates *Capoeira* (a national sport) and the festivities of *Carnaval and Festa Junina (A Summer Harvest).*

8) Russians celebrate *Pagan* holidays as well as Christian. Christians celebrate *Christmas* and *Easter.*

9) The Hindus, Sikhs and Jains celebrate the *Diwali Festival of Lights.* Diwali symbolizes the triumph of good over evil and light over darkness.

10) Muslims celebrate a festival called *Eid Al-Fitr,* which means *Festival of Breaking the Fast.* It's a three day celebration at the end of *Ramadan,* a 30 day dawn-to-sunset fast. It is a time of prayer, sermon, food, gifts, donations, family and the honoring of ancestors. Check online for more specific information.

11) There is a **Slavic Holiday** called *Maslenitsa,* which means *The End of a Harsh Winter.* It is celebrated with blinis, snowball fights, family gatherings and community events. More information can be discovered through a search engine.

12) The Dutch communities (Holland) celebrate the eve *of Saint Nicholas Day or Sinterklaas's Birthday*. Christmas Day, known as Eerste Kerstdag, is more reverent and family-oriented. There are family meals, church services and Christmas stories.

13) People-oriented Holidays (in the U.S.)
You will find these specific and important personal holidays in the section on monthly holidays, but they deserve to be mentioned again so these events don't get lost in the shuffle of other events. Each one will have it's own unique theme: photos, decorations and tributes.

Celebrate President's Day, Martin Luther King Day, Veteran's Day, Mother's Day, and Father's Day.

And, of course, one of the most important people-oriented holidays is your own. Many business owners celebrate their birthdays and other important days at their place of business with cake, flowers and balloons.

Exercise:
1. What ethnic holidays would be interesting, profitable or fun for your business?

2. What religious holidays would be profitable and fun for your business?

* **IMPORTANT:** Do you Badass Growth Hackers have any interesting information you'd like to contribute to this section? Submit it to businessacademy10@aol.com and give us permission to use your submission in our next printing of this book, along with your name and business name. Thank you in advance!

174

USE WHAT YOU LEARNED IN CHAPTER ELEVEN:

HONORING THE RELIGIOUS AND ETHNIC HOLIDAYS
Promotions to Celebrate Cultural Diversity

1. How different religious and ethnic celebrations add meaning to people's lives.
2. How to better understand another culture's way of living in the world.
3. Use what you learned about the 13 religious and ethnic *growth hacks* for growing your business.

Notes:

Notes:

CHAPTER TWELVE:

AVOID THE PAIN
The Facts You Need to Know!

The 13 Deadly Mistakes That Can Destroy an Entrepreneur's First Business: When Failure is Not an Option

I wasn't sure where to insert this chapter since the content is both scary (deadly mistakes) and inspirational (facts and solutions). Owning or running a salon is not without its challenges and you will experience them at some point in your entrepreneurial endeavors. The goal is to be as *prepared as possible* and that is the goal of this chapter. I put this chapter at the end of the book because I didn't want to scare you, but this content is important to know. I recommend you read it so you can avoid some of the pain points that go along with owning your own salon business.

Mistakes and failures are two deadly situations that may cause you immense emotional pain, and to close your salon before it even gets off the ground. They might keep you from having the successful salon you deserve. This chapter is designed to educate you about what mistakes to avoid before you start your first business.

As a serial entrepreneur, I have experience with both of these situations: deadly mistakes and the failure of a business or dream. I wrote this information from personal experience, and as painful as it has been, I don't want you to make the same deadly mistakes. For the most part, I have given examples from my own experiences and trust that you will take heed and steer away from the mistakes that could sabotage your dreams of owning a successful business. Salon ownership is challenging, but also rewarding and enriching. It's a life changing experience you don't want to miss.

As a new entrepreneur, you know the excitement of starting a new business, as well as how much work and effort you'll put into your project. It's your baby, the baby who will grow, change your life and make a difference in your community or even the world.

"That promise or commitment to excellence, to growing a valid business can be exciting, but it can also be trying, especially in the beginning and throughout the transitions. It's all part of the process, and developing your strengths will see you through."

As a first time salon owner you may have to do it all to save money or because you think only you can do it right. You may be inundated with questions, comments etc., regarding your business by outside vendors, employees, friends and family. It can seem over-whelming at first and it is. In time you will learn how to easily handle all the fires that pop up almost on a daily basis.

One of the certainties that will personally happen to you is that your life and your relationships will change, and whether that change is good or not so good is determined by how you perceive and interpret those situations. As a side note, I want to say that even the situations that appear 'not so good' can be 'opportunities for growth.' It's often been said that people learn more from their mistakes than they do from their victories. Allow this guide to help you learn from the mistakes of others so you aren't subjected to unnecessary failures and the unfortunate pain that sometimes goes along with the territory. I trust that this information will be helpful to you in your journey to success.

1) The First Deadly Mistake That Can Destroy an Entrepreneur's First Business is When She/he Fails to Get Clarity Before They Begin

Get Clarity Before You Begin

Starting your own salon is a big move, and there are a lot of decisions, work and money on the line. You must be absolutely certain and clear what your business is about, and what is your message to the public! What is your destination and what is your plan to get there? Get clarity before you start.

I've done it every which way; with a vision, without one and with a vague clarity of where I thought I was going with my new business. For example, when I started my first hair salon in 1975, I had a vague vision of the salon I wanted. The entire industry was in transition and the salon where I worked was not keeping up with the trends. If you're not keeping up, you are falling behind.

Change is a given, and like it or not, you must embrace it. I then made a plan to start my own salon and have it be as professional and up to date as it could be. I didn't buy one blow dryer and ask all my stylists to pass it around. We kept our skills up to date. We knew all the latest styles, and we were well-equipped, and ready to serve anyone who walked through the door. I did really well financially and five years later opened my second salon.

I owned the salons for 14 years altogether before selling and traveling around the world. I then moved out west, where I had my last salon ownership experience. I owned a small salon in a large upscale retirement center where a number of my retired clients had been famous in their careers, or had been married to celebrities. It was a fascinating and wonderful experience that enriched my life in many ways. The elderly were kind, fun, generous and loving to a fault.

It was different with BusinessAcademy.com, my first online

business in the late 1990's. My partner taught sales and I taught marketing to small business owners. I coded a 50 page website, and as a graphic designer, created all the promotional materials. We taught locally in San Francisco and traveled around the country. After our five year partnership ended, the business and website didn't get the attention it needed. My vision had ended and I found it necessary to start again.

Solutions:

It's a big mistake not to do your research. You need to develop an awareness of where your industry is heading. Ask the important questions, "What is new? What is different? Do I have the skills to implement the new ideas? What is holding me back from starting? Do I have the capital for a start up? Do I have the talent or do I need to hire talented people?"

Keep up with trade magazines, thought leaders in your field and read a lot. Go to conferences. Talk to industry insiders about what's next. Just as importantly, educate yourself about social media. It's the king these days in business marketing.

Take your time thinking about it. Seriously, meditate on it. Give yourself some quiet time. Go away for a few days, away from the hustle and bustle and give yourself some time to "be" with your thoughts, ideas and dreams. Make sure you connect with something you're passionate about. Passion will help you in the present and in the future through all the bumps in the road, and they will be there! The important thing is ... get clarity!

One of the most profitable things you can do to stimulate your success is read business books that tell you how to do something right. There are tons of books available written by the experts who have been down the same path and share how they solved their problems.

Sign up for expert online courses at businessacademy10@aol.com. It's a great resource for new business owners. You will find a wealth of information regarding online business courses (where you can learn at home and on your own time), in Business Mastery, Marketing, Social Media and Personal Development. Learn how to make money and be a success through expert guidance.

The world is your oyster, and if you don't get yourself out there and serve customers, somebody else will be happy to do it and take the money. You might be late to the game, but it's not too late. Get out there with something innovative, even if you take an idea from another industry. Go for it! And have that clarity before you start. You can always tweak your business later if necessary.

2) The Second Deadly Mistake That Can Destroy an Entrepreneur's First Business is When She/He Fails to Pre-Plan for Their Business's Future

Pre-Plan for Your Business's Future Success

This mistake comes under the all-important heading of goal setting. You've gotten clarity, and it's time to take the second step. Benjamin Franklin said, *"When you fail to plan, you plan to fail."* There is something to be said for planning your salon step-by-step before you take the journey. Having a roadmap for where you are going helps to reach your destination. By doing so, you know where you are, what there is left to do and when you have reached your first goals. Just like in football, there is a goal post to help the players know that they've reached their goal and made winning points. It works the same for your business.

We're told how to do this via a business plan, which many business owners do and others do not. Many people fly by the seat of their pants and make random decisions to see where it all goes. I don't think there's anything wrong with 'playing it by ear' occasionally. Some project or opportunity may arise and it could (or not) turn out to be something that attracts a new type of client. Many of the promotions I participated in when I had my various businesses were not in my plan, but I went with them anyway. Sometimes you have to be flexible.

Another important part of pre-planning for your business's success is having enough money to make a sincere go of it. Many start up salons begin on a shoestring. Finances are tight, so the salon owner(s) must be creative with their resources. Some salons can get away with that, but many cannot. It isn't long before the salon owner realizes she/he is running out of cash, and can no longer support the salon.

That's why it's so important to write out a business plan and an estimate of what it will cost to maintain the salon for about two years. Various businesses (skin care center, day spa, nail salon, barber shop), will have a shorter or longer lead time, but I found it takes about that amount of time to get established, especially in a brick and mortar store. It may be different online, but there are many costs, even with an online business; websites, hosting, maintenance, domain name costs, computer, monthly internet fees, software, online advertising, graphic design, and all kinds of apps or add-ons can make an online business quite expensive. And you may have inventory/storage costs as well.

Solutions:

Overall, having a 5 and a 10 year plan is a good thing, especially if you have big dreams you want to achieve. For example, let's say you want to own a day spa. You don't have the funding to open the spa of your dreams, but you start with something you can open right away, at a cost you can afford. Maybe it's a small nail or hair salon, or a massage business.

Example: *Let's look at the idea of wanting a Day Spa, but taking it step by step:*

Step One: You could start by first selling spa retail products online to build up your traffic and sales. Drop shipping could be n easy way to fill out your offerings. You offer valuable insight on your blog. You might consider private label products ... unique to you. Maybe you sell through Etsy, Shopify or Amazon? Do your research, and learn which products are desirable and/or necessary to your target market.

Step Two: You eventually get the capital and rent a physical unit to start with a small massage business. If you are the owner/manager of a massage business, you would hire the best people to work in your business. If you are the expert, you would do both ... massage and management. As each year passes, you would incorporate any products/services that would fit into your space, such as retail items, or maybe a manicure table or two. Continue selling product online and promoting your massage business.

Step Three: Sometime before your 5th anniversary, you would start looking for a location to expand your services. You look around your town for a location with several rooms for whatever services you are ready to provide; a hair salon, manicure rooms, retail area, bathrooms and showers, hot tub, wet and dry sauna, swimming pool etc. Choose services that will bring in income and help your dreams to come true. Remember to get feedback from your customers about what they want.

It's a good sign and much to your credit if you make it to the five year mark. This is the time you want to start thinking BIG! Moving from location to location is a lot of work and is very expensive, especially when it comes to installing electrical and plumbing services, along with new equipment. This is your biggest step, so you may need a loan.

I suggest renting or buying a place you can grow into, and plan for how you'll use every bit of space. I was always amazed at how quickly I filled an oversized space. There's a saying "Space abhors a vacuum." This means that if you have extra space, whether it's an empty drawer or an empty room or two (in your business) that space will soon be taken up with something.

Ten years can seem like a long time away, especially when you are just starting out. But time really does fly and all of a sudden the time to make that next move is at your doorstep. After moving into my first hair salon, I looked around and told myself that I would stay there for five years. And it was pretty close to five years when a new shopping center in my town opened up. I saved up a substantial amount of money so when I applied for a unit in the new center, I was prepared.

For example, I was in my twenties when I started my first hair salon on a shoestring. I bought half my used equipment at a garage sale. I bought some new items and some things on consignment from a supply house. Some people don't believe me when I tell them I started up my first salon with $3,000 in 1975. It wasn't ideal, but it was a start, and it paid off. The used equipment looked fine and served me for five years before I moved to a more prestigious location with brand new top of the line equipment (which I saved for). I achieved my vision.

I started small, took baby steps and grew into my *destination*s and goals. Not everyone wants to do that. They want to start at the top. My father wanted to own a sporting goods store with boats, motors, and lots of expensive equipment. I suggested he start small and build up to it. He didn't want to do that, and he died having never had the experience of his own sporting goods store. Don't let your dreams die. Do what you can to start.

3) The Third Deadly Mistake That Can Destroy an Entrepreneur's First Business is When She/he Fails to Have A Marketing Plan to Successfully Promote Their Business

Create a Yearly Marketing Plan

A critical part of any business is having a good marketing plan. It's just as important as a business plan and is always a part of the business plan that will be shown to potential investors.

A marketing plan tells investors, the bank and yourself what you will do to market (promote and advertise) your salon in order to make it successful. They want to know how they will get a return on their investment. This information tells customers what products or services you are selling and why they should buy them or what problem will be solved. They'll learn how you can help them, how you are different from other salons and what they can expect to experience in your salon.

Marketing is a bit more complicated than it once was, but your outreach can be more global. Instead of reaching local consumers, you now have access to the entire world through the internet. That is both the good news and the not so good news. Marketing has gotten more complicated and time consuming, but the rewards are also more significant.

Solutions:

It is now standard business practice to implement all the various types of marketing:

- Personal networking
- Business card referrals
- Local flyers
- Radio and television
- Billboards
- Advertising banners on buses and cars
- Direct mail
- FaceBook
- Twitter
- Pinterest
- Podcasting
- Blogging and vlogging
- Instagram
- Public Relations
- Anything else you can think of that can reach your ideal customer.

Marketing in a Nutshell

1. Be clear on what you are selling.
2. Discover who your audience is and determine what it is they want or are willing to buy? What is the problem you are helping them

with?

3. Clarify your message to your audience. Make sure it's structured in a way that speaks to your audience and gets them to your door or website (See Resources section *"Building a StoryBrand"* by Donald Miller. I highly recommend it).

4. Discover who your competition is, and what they are doing to get customers?

5. Ask yourself how you can differentiate your salon from others in your neighborhood? Send the right message at the right time.

6. Price your product or service appropriately for your target market.

IMPORTANT TIPS:

* Refer to my marketing/promotional books on both traditional and social media marketing. *"How to Organize Your Marketing Campaign; and Hit the Ground Running"* and *"How to Start Up & Manage Your Own Hair Salon ... and Make it BIG in the Salon Business."*

4.) The Fourth Deadly Mistake That Can Destroy an Entrepreneur's First Business is When She/He Fails to Ask Their Customers What They Want

What Problem(s) Will Your Business Solve?

You can't assume you know. If you think you know but you aren't plugged into the current trends then you'll drive very little traffic to your salon. It doesn't matter if you sell online or offline because you don't have the things they want. What are you personally passionate about?

1. What skills/knowledge do you already have that you can transfer to this new career?

2. What personal or professional connections do you have that can help you determine your success?

3. What problems exist for your potential customer, and do you have those solutions?

4. What is your message that will help you drive traffic to your salon business?

5. What is your marketing plan to achieve the success you desire?

*No matter what kind of business you start, answering these questions will help you build rapport with your customers.

Look Around You ... Ask Questions!

There was a popular dress shop downstairs from my first salon. They did well financially for years until all of a sudden they didn't. They sold everything and closed their doors. When I asked why, I was told, *"Who knew denim was going to be so big?"* These older women didn't pay attention to the trends until it was too late. The 1980's were a big time for denim jeans, dresses and jackets. So maybe you carry denim, but customers now want form fitting (yoga) stretch pants. As business owners, we have to be aware of trends.

For another example, let's say you have a passion for jewelry and like to carry beaded jewelry in your showcase. You love it, but what about your local customers? Is that what they are looking for? Does it go with the latest fashion? If not, you will find yourself with a very small market. You can build a website and promote/sell your beaded jewelry on FaceBook, Etsy, Pinterest or Ebay. You might make some money, but you probably won't scale your business like you would if you created something more on trend.

What if you sell handbags in your hair or nail salon, and also sell them online. We all know there is a broad array of handbags, but you have something special and sell it at a high price. Is that your customer, someone who wants a luxury brand? You either need to target those customers or offer a variety of handbags at different price levels.

Solutions:

What are the celebrities, influencers, or high society people wearing? What's showing up in fashion magazines or on the trendy streets of NYC, London or Paris? Grab some attention by offering jewelry, handbags or whatever is either uniquely yours or uniquely someone else's … with your twist. Sometimes it's not what you offer so much as it is about 'how' you offer it … via your presentation or your price point.

If you want to know what customers want, you have to ask them! Interview your customers about your product or service. Or interview friends, family, co-workers or heck … anyone you meet. Where is there a flaw in a product or service that is making customers unhappy? Can you do something about it to make it better?

What about these items are customers unhappy about? What pain are consumers going through that you can help them with? Can you sell beauty supplies at a better price point, or a better brand they can't find locally?

What are your customer's pain points? I did surveys in my business to learn the pain points and/or expectations of my customers.

Listening is a lost art. Listen to what customers are saying, and if you can, follow through with the tips that will keep them coming back for more. People are more into talking and not listening to what others are saying. You learn more when you listen. It's fine to keep your nose to the grindstone, but looking up once in a while is a good thing.

5) The Fifth Deadly Mistake That Can Destroy an Entrepreneur's First Business is When She/He Fails to Nurture or Build Relationships with Customers and Vendors

How Important are Your Business Relationships to You?

What I often see is that some business people and their employees are there only to sell a product or service. That's it, and no other special effort is made to enhance a relationship. I instantly get the feeling that they are thinking, "Buy my product or service and go. I just want your money." I actually see that a lot in the business world, more often in small retail establishments and restaurants. Certain cultures fail to make a personal connection. It's all about "them and their need to take your dollars."

You wouldn't want to do business with someone who you felt was a bit shady would you? Right off the bat you get the idea that at some point you will be taken advantage of or cheated. No one wants that, and when you are new to business, there will be people who come along who seem sincere but are there to take you, cheat you or set up a scheme to be dishonest.

Solutions:

Whatever kind of business you're in is about building relationships, even if you are selling products and not a service. There are people involved at some point, and they are the ones you are in relationship with. Many people underestimate the value and importance of being kind and helpful to others. Relationship building isn't difficult. It's developing an awareness that another's viewpoints, concerns and values are just as important as yours. If you want to do unlimited business with someone, it takes building a relationship based on likeability and trust. I've always been told that people want to do business with someone that they trust. I've also found that when one is a bit more generous than expected it has its merits. Sometimes the favor is returned.

What I'm trying to say here that when you build good relationships with people (customers, vendors, other business owners), when it's time for them to choose who to do business with, your name may come up first because they've experienced your goodwill.

Try to remember that you are not in this alone. You may be a solo-preneur, but you have many different kinds of partners. They may be your vendors, accountant, attorney, landlord, business coach, therapist, doctor or any number of people who are directly or indirectly part of your business or your life.

I mentioned that a couple of employees took products and money, and several times customers did their best to cheat me. A woman and her sister came into the salon and wanted her long dark hair highlighted, cut and styled. It took most of my day to lighten it and complete her services. Highlighting is a complicated and expensive procedure. During one of our conversations she mentioned she was a fortune teller and *"she saw good things for me."* I thanked her, but a red flag popped up in my mind. Toward the end of the day she wanted to talk with me personally and she suggested that she would give me a *reading* in trade for my services. I did not fall for that con game. I told her I was sorry, but I did not have time for a reading in my busy schedule (a 10 min. reading vs. a 4+ hour service). I was kind and forthright. In the meantime her children tore signs off the walls, destroyed our cosmetic counter and ran around untethered. She paid her bill and left.

Hopefully you will see through customers who write bad checks or are dishonest. You want to build good relationships, but not be cheated. People can be shrewd and you need to be strong. There is no training that can help you negotiate with a gypsy fortune teller. It's an unusual situation/relationship that requires you to be on your toes.

6) The Sixth Deadly Mistake That Can Destroy an Entrepreneur's First Business is When She/He Fails to Carefully Choose Their Employees

Choose Employees Wisely:

When you have the money or the need for employees, it can seem like the best thing in the world. You need the help, and it shows the world that you and your business are growing. And naturally, that could mean more profits. There's nothing nicer than having other people take up the slack and give you extra time to do other things that need to be done. It's a big mistake to not have employees you can trust.

190

Employees bring both joy and sometimes challenges. The joy is in the support they may offer, and in the good times that are shared. It's nice to have people to talk to about new products or services or the various aspects of your salon. Really good employees can enrich your life, and help make your salon more profitable. You will share in each other's rewarding life experiences.

But it isn't all rosy, and sometimes employees make critical errors and become dysfunctional. They have family disturbances that play a part in your salon, just as much as if that person were a spouse or partner. You may have to deal with everything they deal with on a daily basis. Their problems are your problems: sick children, divorce, breakups, health challenges etc. And the smaller your business is the more you are susceptible.

Some employees are not trustworthy. They steal from you, and you may or may not be aware of it. I'm not going to say it happens to every salon or spa owner, but theft is probably more common than we think, whether it's money or products. It happens to small business owners as well as large corporations.

I remember reading a book written by a famous motivational speaker who was heartbroken when his (financial assistant) had taken a lot of money from his bank account. It was someone he trusted, and he didn't know the money was gone until it was all over. Thieves are shrewd and will make sure you don't catch them in the act.

I once caught an employee who stole a costly retail item from my business. I left the business before her. I was outside scraping the snow off my car when she came out carrying the item she had taken. I was shocked and hurt, as I never expected that kind of behavior from her.

Solutions:

In my book *"How to Organize Your Marketing Campaign"* I offer a set of questions to use when interviewing potential employees. You may want to do background checks, especially when someone tries to hide their background. You can even check into their history online for a fee.

You can't always go by that and know who is honest and forthright and who is not. People change and their circumstances change. They do things they would not otherwise do, like take money from a cash drawer. Unless you really don't care about money, I encourage you to keep your eyes open, check the numbers and follow up on accounting.

7) The Seventh Deadly Mistake That Can Destroy an Entrepreneur's First Business is When She/He Fails to Look Around to See if Employees are Happy

Do You Care as Much About Others' Happiness as You Do About Your Own?

I once read that the reason many employees quit their place of employment is because they are unhappy. If you look around your workplace and don't see people with happy, smiling faces (at least part of the time), then your business might be in trouble. What I mean by 'being in trouble' is that you might lose a valued employee that you would dearly like to keep. If that person's work is a crucial part of your income, then you really need to listen up.

Maybe they are your best salesperson or your best hairstylist, manicurist, massage therapist, or whatever. If that person's value or worth to you as an employee appears to be jeopardized, then you need to find out why.

1. Are they having personal problems?
2. Is their problem work-related?
3. Are they not getting along with someone?
4. Have they lost their passion?
5. Do they want more money?
6. Do they want to live in a more desirable area, or to be closer to loved ones?
7. Are they leaving for personal growth reasons?

Maybe they've grown as much as they can at your business and feel they can learn more or up their game elsewhere. It's become a natural part of growing one's career opportunities. Employees no longer stay with the same company and retire after 30 years.

Usually, but not always, there are signs when someone is unhappy and it's often demonstrated through attitude. Someone may sulk, show anger or frustration or *act out* in some negative way. Their challenge might be a health issue or a family issue or an important disagreement with another employee. Sexual harassment can be a problem in the workplace.

There is a critical importance in discovering a problem in your workplace and facilitating a solution. The last thing you want is for more than one person to leave because of workplace issues that were not resolved.

Get your head out of the sand, and start finding solutions to inspire more joy in your salon or spa. Workplace issues can be resolved through mediation. Don't be afraid to call someone to get your business back to a place of peace and joy.

Solutions:
Look at your business from their perspective and not yours. There are a number of things that may keep your workplace on an even keel. You might want to have a heart to heart chat with employees to find out if they can be helped or offered positive advice.

Find team building ideas to implement. Have *after hours* events so employees can bond and perhaps even contribute to increasing rapport. Discover ways to keep employees interested, creative, and maybe even entertained. Have contests, parties, celebrations, advanced education, certificates of appreciation and/or use any ideas in this book. Make your salon a place where employees can earn money, grow professionally, creatively and have a joyful time.

8) The Eighth Deadly Mistake That Can Destroy an Entrepreneur's First Business is When She/He Fails to Have a Support System in

Place

Create a Positive Support System

When you go into business, the magic number is two. It really does take two to be successful. Whether that other person is a partner, spouse, family member, a mentor/coach, or a supportive employee, it's always best to have a support person as an important part of your team. You'll have someone to bounce ideas off of or to help you from making mistakes that you might regret.

However well prepared or educated you think you are, you can never know what lies ahead and how to handle surprises that show up in your salon. It throws you off when customers or even employees fool you or behave in ways in which you are unprepared. No one can teach you how to handle every problem. MBA's and CEO's make mistakes too. Read or listen to the business news, and you will see how many errors and misjudgments they make.

You have to use your intuition and also stay tactful. Almost every day is a learning experience. Take the not so good with the good because both can be valuable life lessons.

Solutions:

Owning and operating a salon business by yourself is a mighty challenge. There are lots of hats to wear and you can't be good at everything or do it all … no matter how hard you try. There will always be someone else who can do something better. Maybe they sell better, or cut hair better or market better or are better organized. Learn your strengths and weaknesses and find people or an individual who can be better at what you cannot do. Absorb the support, but also give back when they need a hand to hold.

Having someone to talk to like a coach, mentor, therapist, attorney, minister, or a business support group can be very helpful or comforting when you find yourself backed up against the wall, in tears, ready to have a nervous breakdown or tearing your hair out over some issue (that you won't even remember two months later).

Find someone to share your turmoil's with, also remembering to listen to their challenges. Giving each other feedback and support will help you both with correct perceptions and the stamina to stay in business while expressing your passion and reaching your dreams.

9) The Ninth Deadly Mistake That Can Destroy an Entrepreneur's First Business is When She/He Fails to Set Boundaries

Learn How to Set Boundaries

Learning how to set boundaries can help with reducing entrepreneurial burnout. The time you dedicate to making your salon work is important and should not be interrupted. There is power in saying "no" and meaning it. I found, in my startup stages, that I had to sacrifice social and family time to spend more time with getting my salons off the ground. That's the decision you make when you decide for a startup. Unless you have a lot of money to pay other people to take care of things for you, it all falls on your shoulders, and that can be a heavy burden at times. Since startups do not become big overnight, you will most likely take a couple years to reach your vision.

While you are in the process of growing your salon, there will be demands on your time from outside vendors, co-workers, family members and the general public. There are many moving parts, like the inside of a watch, and because you have elected to coordinate those moving parts, it can be an overwhelming experience. If you have a problem saying *"no"* to people, then you have a problem.

Solutions:

It doesn't matter if you become a one person hair salon owner or a solo-preneur who owns the day spa down the street from Facebook. To set boundaries is to protect your territory, whether it's the territory of business functionality or territory around your personal or social life. Your duties and responsibilities to business and family work best by drawing a line where your time is concerned. Setting boundaries protects you from interruptions that may make or break your ability to succeed.

When I am focused on writing, I turn the sound off on my computer so I don't hear email coming in to interrupt my chain of thought. Here are some ideas for *drawing the line:*

- Turn off the sound on your email if you don't want your thoughts to be interrupted.
- Turn off the sound on social media platforms.
- Turn off the ringing of your phones.
- Set boundaries around your work time. Tell people in advance when you are not available to chat or discuss social events.
- Make appointments to talk when it is convenient for you.
- Say *no* when you must.

10) The Ninth Deadly Mistake That Can Destroy an Entrepreneur's First Business is When She/He Fails to Get Feedback or Critiques

Getting Feedback Helps You Stay on Course

It's during your start up phase that you most need feedback or critiques from a mentor, a coach, a mastermind group or anyone in your field or industry who has more experience than you.

Unless you've gained a lot of experience through other business ventures, it's easy to make wrong decisions or decisions that are not in your best interests. Get feedback on the effectiveness of your website, marketing materials, business cards or anything that feels uncertain.

For instance, let's say you want to open an online beauty supply store, then eventually a brick and mortar store. You know who your customer is and what they want to buy. You then research what your competition is selling and what the trends are right now. You offer your products at a price your customer is willing to pay, and also consider an up-sell. As long as everything is in alignment you should be able to make sales.

When sales are off, then you need to go back to square one and find out why. Ask yourself these important questions. Have styles changed? Are you charging too much for in comparison to other online stores? Is another business offering something extra? Get feedback from venders or suppliers. They can give you a clue as to what owners of successful beauty supply stores are doing.

Solutions:

I always ask for feedback or a critique, whether I am building a website, or writing a book. When I built a website for BusinessAcademy. com, I sent out a posting to my local networking group, asking for an honest critique. Two people replied that it was too busy and too hard to read. I took their feedback to heart and reworked it until it was simpler for the customer to understand.

If anything can be done *just a little bit better* you want to know about it because you want your work or effort to be the best it can be. I too, have a coach that I check in with on a regular basis. In fact we help each other on almost all of our projects. It's just a good business practice, and can help your business stay alive.

11) The Eleventh Deadly Mistake That Can Destroy an Entrepreneur's First Business is When She/He Fails to Take Risks

Be Selective When Taking Risks

As a serial entrepreneur, I consider myself well-versed in starting up small businesses and facing risks. Some of my businesses have been successful and some have not. What I've learned is that sometimes you have to take risks, and other times it is better or safer not to. How do you know when to take risks and when to play it safe?

If you want to play it safe, just keep your day job. But is keeping your day job safe? Not really! You can get laid off and have to start again. Then it's about looking for another job, adjusting to a learning curve and a new work culture. I worked for two non-profits as a graphic designer and administrative assistant in my long career. Statewide budget cuts caused me to experience several layoffs. There was no job security there.

You can always think you are playing it safe, but at some point change happens. Internet platforms change their algorithms and there goes your business and profits. It's a part of life and we must do the best we can. It's sort of like "thinking on your feet." You have to be ready to switch perceptions and actions when it is in your best interests to do so.

There's no formula for when to take a risk and when to stay put.
1. You can take small risks with small amounts of capital. Try it out and see how much fear comes up for you. It's sort of like investing in the stock market. Start out small and take larger risks as you get a better sense of the market and become more comfortable with losing or gaining money. Should you add a manicurist to your day spa? Ask your customers if they would use that service, or do they already have a favorite nail salon. Then you know.

2. You can do research and talk to people who have critical information on what fields or industries are doing well and which ones are not. See if it's a match.

3. Interview someone who has already accomplished your goal. Ask how to be a success in that business or how that person became successful?

4. There are also books on almost every industry. What I've found is that you can't always go by that either. It's a guessing game really, and what works for one will not always work for another. There are just too many variables.

I'm going to go out on a limb here and say that we must take risks and sometimes they pay off and sometimes they don't. You will learn just as much from your failures as you do from your successes, and you'll take those lessons with you on your next adventure.

As painful as it was, I'm going to reveal my experience of trying to break into the nail salon industry, for which I failed badly. You can take this example and apply it to any business that excites you.

Many years ago when I started my second hair salon in Indiana, I decided to expand my manicure and pedicure services, and hired an extra person to offer that service. Well, the truth is I couldn't even give away that service. Why? After all the marketing and promos I did, (and freebies) I just couldn't figure out why those services didn't sell. My business was in a shopping center in a great location, and still no sales. No other businesses in the area were doing nail services and I thought it would be a needed and helpful service. Many years later I realized I was just too early. It wasn't a trend at that time. I often wish I had all the money I threw away on that project.

Nowadays, nail salons are booming. They are often booked solid. Of course, I no longer have a salon so I can't cash in on the boom. And now that I have additional information, I would still not take on that risk. You'll learn why.

Many years later, when nail salons were just starting to become popular in California ... I saw two opportunities. I had a friend who was retiring and she wanted to start a small business, something easy to operate. I suggested a nail salon. Since she had the capital and I had the management and start up experience, I offered to help set up a small nail salon, manage and promote it. We would both make a little side income. After much discussion she decided not to move forward. She was playing it safe, and I could understand her position.

Some years after that, I started a little side-line business offering spa parties at home for Ladies Pampering Night and Bachelorette parties. I got everything lined up for the parties except the mani/pedi part. I couldn't get anyone local to come out and earn the extra money with the potential to get new customers. I heard lots of excuses. I finally found a student who helped out one evening. She worked too slow, and I had to do most of the mani-pedi's. I wasn't expecting to be bogged down with that work since I was also coordinating the event. I eventually gave up the project. Fortunately it wasn't at a financial loss, but at a loss to what I thought was an opportunity.

This challenge with nail services continued for another salon for seniors I owned some years later. I realized then that the industry is owned (at least in California) by young Asian and South East Asian women, and they don't want to work for anyone else. So my co-worker and I continued to do manicures at the expense of higher priced services, because our customers needed them.

When I realized I was beating a dead horse, I was glad that I didn't push my retired friend to invest her hard earned money into a nail salon. We probably would have struggled and we would have lost our investment of money, time and energy. On the other hand we might have been lucky enough to find good employees but after all those failures it was a risk I didn't want to take. What eventually became clear to me is that a mani-pedi business was not part of my destiny. That door just didn't open for me. You may find that too, and if so, it's best to try another door.

Solutions:

Sometimes the success of a small personal service or retail business depends on the personality of the owner. Ask yourself if you have the social skills necessary to work with the general public? Are you likeable, tactful, diplomatic and patient with people? Those are the people skills you need beyond marketing and business skills.

When it comes to choosing a start up salon business, and deciding whether to take a risk or play it safe, I recommend several options besides rereading this book. To value your investment, do this:

1. Do plenty of research. Take a course or buy a book on the industry or field.

2. Talk to people in your industry and ask the critical questions to get the whole story. What are the pros and cons?

3. Find out the costs and if the money you have is substantial enough to support your salon for at least a couple of years.

4. Ask yourself if it really is your passion or just something you want to invest in to make side money? Your passion will get you further than a passing interest. You can always depend on yourself, but not always on outsiders. Remember, I was able to do mani-pedis when I couldn't find a manicurist.

5. Can you scale your salon business? Discern if it will grow enough to give you a good income for yourself and some employees? Are others making a profit? Can you make a profit?

6. Research how well your competition is doing and if you can surpass them.

***

Remember that many companies operate for years without making a profit. Amazon and Tesla are two well-known examples. Sometimes it just takes *time* before your salon will get off the ground. You have to be able to either *hold out* for a while or *cut your losses* and bail.

Think about your plan and your goals. Do you have a five-year plan to add a new service or move to a more booming area or take your business online? If so, the risk might be right for you, especially if you have enough finances and resources. Ask yourself how badly you want to take a risk? Will you be okay if you fail or if you win? Will a win be a major deal for your business? You may not know until you try, and if you do try it might take time to get where you want to be. Again, weigh the pro's and con's, and follow your heart.

12) The Twelfth Deadly Mistake That Can Destroy an Entrepreneur's First Business is When She/He Overworks and Fails to Engage in Self Care

Remember That You are a Big Part of the Equation

In the first years of your new start up, you will spend a lot of time getting all the moving parts to fit together ... like a finely tuned watch.

A lot of hours are spent on the start procedures and paperwork, website, brick and mortar salon and marketing. It doesn't matter if your business is primarily online or offline or both. You are looking for vendors, building your email list, creating content, connecting with other business owners and on and on. All of this work can lead to burnout if you don't take time to de-stress.

If you find yourself always in an emotional state of turmoil over something regarding your salon, you may have the beginning stages of burnout. In business, things don't always go right or in the time frame you anticipated. It's just part of the process. You may have to adjust your plan, taking into account the bumps in the road that are a part of the salon business.

Sometimes things move too fast and you are unprepared. Being unprepared can cause a loss of sales too. If you watch Shark Tank on television you will discover that some businesses get more sales than they can handle. They don't have the money to invest in more supplies or enough employees to take care of the influx of new customers. Watching this show will give you some ideas on how businesses start up, what their problems are and potentially how they are solved. Let it be a learning experience and learn from another's mistakes and victories.

Solutions:

The solution for this twelfth mistake is to take care of yourself. Here are my first ideas:

1. When possible, give yourself some time off. Take a vacation of a few days or a week away just to relax.

2. Ask someone else to fill in for you for a day or two. You come back rejuvenated and ready to take on tasks with renewed energy.

3. If you really can't get away for at least a weekend, go to a local resort or go camping or play golf or mini-golf to refresh yourself.

4. Take a yoga class or learn meditation or mindfulness to help focus on your inner peace rather than anything related to business.

Sometimes focusing within rather than on those same old problems will give you needed insight.

5. It's a revealing experience to talk to a hypnotherapist or therapist to get worries off your chest. Have you explored alternative healing and had no promising results? It may take more than one session to find relief.

6. The next step is to see a medical doctor or an alternate health practitioner, especially if you are complaining of neck or shoulder pain from stress.

7. If you haven't physically injured yourself (or even if you have) chronic pain can be a sign of burnout or psychosomatic pain. The body is a communication device and has a way of letting us know when something is off physically, emotionally or spiritually. If we have any kind of body awareness, we notice when something is amiss in our bodies, and we must listen. The communication is ultimately pointing us in the direction of healing. What it tells you is up to your interpretation, but seeing a medical practitioner is a good next step.

If the medical community can't solve your issues and alleviate your pain or burnout, I'll make a radical suggestion that the problem may be one of *faulty perceptions.* Is there something or someone that you need to forgive? Could it be yourself? Maybe you need to make a lifestyle change, especially if you have burned out and your physical or emotional pain has become too much? There's nothing wrong with letting go and starting a new chapter of your life.

13) The Thirteenth Deadly Mistake That Can Destroy an Entrepreneur's First Business is in When She/he Fails to Recognize When Family Relationships are Suffering

Keep Family Close to Your Heart

The last important mistake that first time business owners often make is in not nurturing family members. You are on this business journey together and they should know it from the start. You will spend a lot of time at or with your salon, and since there are only so many hours in the day, something will need to give. It will most likely be time with family and/or loved ones. They will just not get as much of you as they previously did, so that could cause them to feel unloved, unneeded or even unnecessary. Don't let that happen because they are your anchors in a safe port and your most important support system.

The last thing you want to do is brush your family aside because of your new start up. If your children are acting out or your husband/wife or sweetheart is behaving unenthusiastically, it's time to take notice and make some changes. It's in everyone's best interests for them to become more engaged and supportive of you in your new or continuing business venture.

Solutions:

Acknowledge to yourself first that you need them, their support and their presence in your life. They make you happy on many levels and to have them there for you is a powerful measure of your success. You'll sleep better at night knowing that your family is there for you no matter what happens in your salon or how long it takes to get it off the ground.

Secondly, acknowledge to your family that they are an important part of your salon, even if they don't physically participate in the running of your salon or spa. Include family members in your business decisions, so they feel they are contributing to your success. Your success is their success, especially when your income increases and they see the benefits of supporting you.

Let family play a part in your salon if they want to and if the situation allows. Pay them to participate. I hired my sister to clean my salon, and I hired my mother to answer the phone and do menial tasks. Let them be your unofficial board of directors and help make decisions or even give feedback on problems. You never know when children or your spouse may come up with creative ideas and solve a particular problem. Stay open to how this could evolve.

* "Thank you for allowing me to share what I feel *are the most important mistakes you can make in your startup business. I wish you all the joyful times that are a part of having your own business.*"

USE WHAT YOU LEARN IN CHAPTER TWELVE: AVOID THE PAIN, The Facts You Need to Know

1. There are mistakes that can be avoided!
2. There are solutions to every problem in these 13 *growth hacks* to grow your business and keep it alive for many years to come.

Badass Important Tip #15: Post a Review!
Before I let you I go, I would like to encourage you to post an honest review on Amazon.com or wherever you purchased this book. Share what you liked. I appreciate it. Visit www.BusinessAcademy.com for essential blog content and great online courses that can shed light on ways to *"Transform Your Salon Into A Badass Money Machine!"* Sign up for our enewsletter to stay in the loop about new courses, freebies and other goodies.
Thank you!

The best to you,
Linda Chappo
Chappo Enterprises

Email: businessacademy10@aol.com
www.BusinessAcademy.com

RESOURCE SECTION:

www.quicksprout.com to learn more about *growth hacking,* and lots of great tips and resources. I recommend you get on this email list.

RECOMMENDED BOOKS:

"BUILDING A STORYBRAND; Clarify Your Message so Customers Will Listen" by Donald Miller

"Crushing it; How Great Entrepreneurs Build Their Business and Influence – and How You Can Too" by Gary Vaynerchuk

"Selfie Made; Your Ultimate Guide to Social Media Stardom" by Meridith Valiando Rojas

"The Everything Guide to Social Media; All You Need to Know About Participating in Today's Most Popular Online Communities" by John K. Waters

"30 Days to Social Media Success; The 30 Day Results Guide to Making the Most of Twitter, Blogging, LinkedIn, and Facebook " by Gail Z.Martin

"Content Rules; How to Create Killer Blogs, Podcasts, Videos, EBooks, Webinars that Engage Customers and Ignite Your Business" by Ann Handley and C.C. Chapman.

Recommended Online Learning Experiences

Thank you for completing this training course. As a special gift, here is the Creativelive link for free online classes:
Check Out CreativeLive's Free On-Air Classes

www.ingramcontent.com/pod-product-compliance
Lightning Source LLC
Chambersburg PA
CBHW031837090426
42741CB00005B/271